KS3
Spanish

Complete Revision
and Practice

Contents

Contents

Published by CGP

Editors:
Heather Gregson
Rachel Grocott
Sabrina Robinson

Contributors:
Janice Crossfield
Deborah McNee
Graham Whittaker

With thanks to Emma Warhurst and Amy Bates for the proofreading.

Audio CD produced by Naomi Laredo of Small Print and recorded, edited and mastered at The Speech Recording Studio by Graham C. Williams, featuring the voices of Carmen Alcántara Fernandez, Andrea Jiménez Garcia, Alejandro Postigo and Alejandro Rodríguez Peña.

ISBN: 978 1 84762 888 6
Website: www.cgpbooks.co.uk
Printed by Elanders Ltd, Newcastle upon Tyne.
Clipart from CorelDRAW®

Based on the classic CGP style created by Richard Parsons.

Numbers

Welcome to <u>KS3 Spanish</u>. Let's start with the <u>basics</u> — <u>numbers</u>.

Learn **the numbers — los números**

Numbers are pretty <u>straightforward</u> and <u>really useful</u>. Make sure you learn them <u>well</u>.

1	2	3	4	5	6	7	8	9	10
uno	*dos*	*tres*	*cuatro*	*cinco*	*seis*	*siete*	*ocho*	*nueve*	*diez*

11 to 15 all end in "<u>ce</u>". But 16, 17, 18 and 19 are "<u>ten and six</u>", etc.

11	12	13	14	15	16	17	18	19
once	*doce*	*trece*	*catorce*	*quince*	*dieciséis*	*diecisiete*	*dieciocho*	*diecinueve*

Most "ten-type" numbers end in "<u>nta</u>" (except "<u>veinte</u>"). "<u>Cien</u>" (100) becomes "<u>ciento</u>" when it's followed by <u>another number</u> — e.g. ciento veinte = 120.

20	30	40	50	60	70	80	90	100
veinte	*treinta*	*cuarenta*	*cincuenta*	*sesenta*	*setenta*	*ochenta*	*noventa*	*cien*

All <u>twenty-something</u> numbers are rolled into one.

21	22	23
veintiuno	*veintidós*	*veintitrés*

After <u>thirty</u>, numbers are joined by "<u>y</u>" (and), but written <u>separately</u>.

31	32	33
treinta y uno	*treinta y dos*	*treinta y tres*

First, **second**, **third** are a bit different

These usually end in "o" for <u>masculine things</u> or "a" for <u>feminine things</u> (see p.111).

1st	2nd	3rd	4th	5th
primero/a	*segundo/a*	*tercero/a*	*cuarto/a*	*quinto/a*

Numbers are a great place to start

Numbers come up loads, from saying when your birthday is to telling your friend what time you'd like to meet. Make sure you know them well and you'll be off to a great start.

Time

Now you know the <u>numbers</u>, put them into <u>practice</u> by learning how to <u>tell the time</u>.

What time is it? — ¿Qué hora es?

This is the <u>question</u> followed by how to <u>answer</u> it: **¿Qué hora es?** = What time is it?

1) SOMETHING O'CLOCK:

Es la una = <u>It's</u> one o'clock   **Son las tres** = <u>It's</u> three o'clock

If it's <u>one o'clock</u> (or to do with one o'clock), you say "<u>es</u> la una", but for every <u>other time</u>, it's "<u>son</u>..."

2) SOMETHING PAST:

Son las dos y cuarto = It's <u>quarter past</u> two

Son las dos y media = It's <u>half past</u> two

To say any minutes past the hour, use "<u>y</u>" (and). This means "it's two <u>and</u> twenty (minutes)".

Son las dos y veinte = It's <u>twenty past</u> two

3) SOMETHING TO:

Es la una menos diez = It's <u>ten to</u> one   **Son las dos menos cinco** = It's <u>five to</u> two

When you use "<u>menos</u>" it's like saying the hour "<u>minus</u>" the <u>number of minutes</u>.

At ten o'clock — A las diez

To say "<u>at something o'clock</u>", you say:

A las + TIME

"<u>Las</u>" changes to "<u>la</u>" for "<u>a la una</u>" (<u>at one o'clock</u>).

A las seis = At <u>six</u> o'clock   **A la una y media** = At half past <u>one</u>

Remember — "es la una menos cinco" is like "it's one minus five"
Telling the time isn't too difficult. First off, remember how to use "menos". Next, learn that to say "something past" you just say the hour "and" (y) the amount of minutes. Not too tricky.

Times and Dates

Knowing different <u>times of day</u> and the <u>days of the week</u> is really handy for loads of things, like <u>arranging to meet people</u> or talking about which <u>activities</u> you do on <u>which days</u>.

Other times — **yesterday**, **today**, **tomorrow**

Here's some vocab for <u>different times</u>:

el día = day   **la mañana** = morning   **ayer** = yesterday

la semana = week   **la tarde** = afternoon/evening   **hoy** = today

el mes = month   **la noche** = night   **mañana** = tomorrow

el año = year

Remember: "la mañana" (morning) and "mañana" (tomorrow) are different.

Days of the week

<u>Days of the week</u> in Spanish <u>don't</u> start with <u>capital letters</u> like they do in English.

lunes — Monday   **martes** — Tuesday   **miércoles** — Wednesday   **jueves** — Thursday   **viernes** — Friday

The days of the week are all masculine.

sábado — Saturday   **domingo** — Sunday   **el fin de semana** — the weekend

To say "<u>on Monday</u>", you put "<u>el</u>" <u>before</u> the <u>day</u>:

¿Quieres ir al cine el lunes? = Do you want to go to the cinema <u>on Monday</u>?

To say what you do "<u>on Mondays</u>", you put "<u>los</u>" <u>before</u> the <u>day</u>:

Los lunes, juego al fútbol. = <u>On Mondays</u>, I play football.

Time flies when you're having fun

You'll use times and days loads in KS3 Spanish. Learn the days of the week so that when you get to p.65-68, you'll be able to say what you do each day. Learn them today, not tomorrow.

Times and Dates

The months in Spanish are important, especially for telling people what date your birthday is.

Months of the year

Months don't start with a capital letter in Spanish and they're all masculine.

enero = January	**mayo** = May	**septiembre** = September
febrero = February	**junio** = June	**octubre** = October
marzo = March	**julio** = July	**noviembre** = November
abril = April	**agosto** = August	**diciembre** = December

Saying the date

Dates will come in very handy when you want to book a holiday (p.90) or meet a friend (p.73).

1) In Spanish, they don't say "the third of May" — they say "the three of May".

    el tres de mayo = the third of May

2) "The first of" is the odd one out:

    el primero de mayo = the first of May

3) This is how you write the date in a letter:

    5 de junio, 2013 = 5th of June 2013

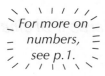

For more on numbers, see p.1.

4) Say when your birthday is:

    Mi cumpleaños es el trece de septiembre. = My birthday is the 13th of September.

Take your time learning months and dates

Learning how to say the date can get a bit boring, but just remember — it'll be useful for loads of things. Dates in Spanish aren't too different from dates in English, so it's pretty easy really.

Practice Questions

Track 1

Listening Question

1   Listen to these people (a-f) telling the time in Spanish, then write
     down the number of the clock face that shows the same time.
     For example: a) Clock 2

1

2

3

4

5

6

2   Write out the sums in words, in Spanish.
     For example: 9 + 10 = 19 *nueve + diez = diecinueve*

   a) 3 + 2 = 5   d) 18 + 2 = 20

   b) 7 − 1 = 6   e) 14 − 13 = 1

   c) 8 + 4 = 12   f) 15 − 2 = 13

3   Write out these words in English.

   a) viernes   d) jueves   g) los viernes

   b) domingo   e) martes   h) lunes

   c) miércoles   f) sábado   i) el fin de semana

4   Write the following dates in Spanish.

   a) 17th September   d) 2nd March

   b) 22nd November   e) 21st July

   c) 14th June   f) 1st January

Meeting and Greeting

Greet someone in Spanish and it will get your conversation off to a great start.

Hello! — ¡Hola!

It's fine to say "hola" (hello) to greet someone.
Depending on the time of day, you can also use these phrases:

Watch out: it's "buenos días" but "buenas tardes" and "buenas noches".

Buenos días

= Good day

Buenas tardes

= Good afternoon/evening

Buenas noches

= Good night

Goodbye! — ¡Adiós!

¡Adiós!

= Goodbye!

¡Hasta pronto!

= See you soon!

¡Hasta luego!

= See you later!

How are you? — ¿Qué tal?

There are a few ways to ask how someone is in Spanish — learn them all.

(1)   **¿Qué tal?**   = How are you?

(2)   **¿Cómo estás?**   = How are you? ⬅ For talking to a friend or a family member.

(3)   **¿Cómo está?**   = How are you? ⬅ For talking to an adult or stranger.
This version is more formal.

Use this to reply and say how you're feeling: **Bien, gracias.**   = (I'm) fine thanks.

See p.29-30 if you're not well and need to explain why.

> *very well:* muy bien
> *not very well:* no muy bien
> *terrible:* fatal

'Hello' isn't the only way you can greet someone

There are a few options here, but they're all pretty straightforward. Make sure you remember how to ask someone how they are and to use the formal version for an adult or stranger.

Meeting and Greeting

Learn how to <u>introduce someone</u> — you <u>don't</u> want to be <u>antisocial</u>.

Let me introduce... — **Le presento a...**

This is for <u>formal</u> introductions. Use it to introduce someone to an <u>adult</u> or <u>stranger</u>.

Le presento a *mi madre.* = Let me introduce <u>my mother</u>.

Put any of the <u>people</u> from <u>p.15</u> in here.

Le presento a *mi amigo.*
Se llama Ben.

= Let me introduce <u>my friend</u>.
His name is Ben.

You can add some details about the person you're introducing.

This is... — **Este es / Esta es...**

This is for <u>informal</u> introductions — use it for introducing people to <u>friends</u> or <u>family</u>.

Este es *Juan.* = <u>This is</u> Juan.
Use this one to introduce a <u>boy</u>.

Esta es *Sara.* = <u>This is</u> Sara.
Use this one to introduce a <u>girl</u>.

Pleased to meet you — **Mucho gusto**

Now you've been <u>introduced</u>, you need to say "<u>pleased to meet you</u>".
There are a couple of ways:

Mucho gusto. = Pleased to meet you.

*Encanta**do**.* = Pleased to meet you.
Use this one if <u>you're a boy</u>.

*Encanta**da**.* = Pleased to meet you.
Use this one if <u>you're a girl</u>.

Have some manners and learn to be polite

You need to learn both the formal and informal ways to introduce someone. Don't forget
"pleased to meet you" — that way you can make some Spanish friends <u>and</u> be polite.

Being Polite

"Please" and "thank you" will help you be polite in all situations. Don't forget to use them.

Please, thank you — por favor, gracias

1) Learn how to say "please":

por favor = please   **La cuenta, por favor.** = The bill, please.

2) This is how to say "thank you":

gracias = thank you   **muchas gracias** = thank you very much

3) If someone says "thank you", say "you're welcome":   **de nada** = you're welcome

There's a polite "you" in Spanish

If you want to be extra polite in Spanish, there's a formal way of saying "you".

1) Spanish people use the informal "you" for talking to a friend or family member:

¿Qué quieres comer? = What do you want to eat?

Informal "you".

2) They use the polite "you" for someone they don't know well, e.g. a waiter in a restaurant:

¿Qué quiere comer? = What do you want to eat?

For more on verb forms, see p.120-124.

Polite "you"— this "you" follows the same pattern as the "he/she/it" form of the verb.

¿Tiene una habitación libre? = Do you have any free rooms?

You'll come across the polite "you" on pages about booking a hotel room or going to the doctor.

Use the formal 'you' to be extra polite to strangers

Basic manners in Spanish are really important and they make you sound more polite.
Knowing when to use the polite 'you' (with adults you don't know well) will helps loads too.

Being Polite

You'll probably have to <u>apologise</u> at some point in your life. Here's how.

I'm sorry — Lo siento

Here are a <u>couple</u> of ways to say you're <u>sorry</u>:

lo siento = I'm sorry   **lo siento mucho** = I'm really sorry

Excuse me — Perdone

These are the <u>different types</u> of "<u>excuse me</u>" you need to know.

1) If you're in the street and want to <u>ask the way</u> or <u>attract</u> someone's <u>attention</u>:

¡Perdone, señora! = Excuse me, <u>madam</u>! ← *When people are talking to each other in <u>formal situations</u> you might hear them say "<u>señor</u>" or "<u>señora</u>".*

sir: señor

You can use <u>this one</u> too: **¡Por favor!** = Excuse me!

2) If someone's <u>in the way</u> and you want to <u>get past</u>:   **¡Con permiso!** = Excuse me!

Yes, no — sí, no

You won't get very far without "<u>yes</u>" and "<u>no</u>" so learn them now.

sí = yes   **no** = no

And to be <u>extra polite</u>:   **Sí, por favor.** = Yes, please.   **No, gracias.** = No, thank you.

I'm sorry but you need to learn this in order to be polite

Don't push someone out of your way in a busy street — it's not polite, no matter where you are in the world. Learn how to say "excuse me" in Spanish and then you'll have no need to be rude.

Being Polite

This page is about saying <u>what you want</u>, as <u>politely</u> as possible.

I would like... — Quisiera...

It's much more polite to say "<u>quisiera</u>" (I would like) than "<u>quiero</u>" (I want).

1) Here's how to say you would like <u>something</u>:

Quisiera un zumo de naranja. = I would like <u>an orange juice</u>.

Quisiera un bocadillo de queso. = I would like <u>a cheese sandwich</u>.

2) Here's how to say you would like <u>to do</u> something:

Quisiera + INFINITIVE

For more on the infinitive, see p.120.

Quisiera hablar. = I would like <u>to talk</u>.

These verbs need to <u>stay</u> in the <u>infinitive form</u>.

Quisiera ir a la piscina. = I would like <u>to go</u> to the swimming pool.

May I...? — ¿Puedo...?

To ask for things politely, you can use "<u>puedo</u>".

Again, this verb has to <u>stay</u> in the <u>infinitive form</u>.

¿Puedo + INFINITIVE?

¿Puedo escuchar la radio? = May I <u>listen</u> to the radio?

go to the toilet: ir al baño
wash the dishes: lavar los platos

Learn this page so you can politely ask people things

If you need to ask your Spanish teacher if you can go to the toilet, don't ask in English — learn how to say it the Spanish way. "¿Puedo ir al baño?" sounds far more impressive.

Practice Questions

Track 2 Listening Question

1 Listen to this conversation at a party and then write down whether each statement is true or false.

   a) Roberto does not feel very well.

   b) Cristina is very well.

   c) Roberto would like something to drink.

   d) Roberto apologises because he does not like cakes.

   e) Roberto says he would like an apple.

2 Choose an expression from the box that you'd be most likely to use in the following situations. Use each expression once.

   a) You are about to go upstairs to bed.

   b) You meet your teacher in town in the afternoon.

   c) You say goodbye to your friend who you'll see later.

   d) You ask your brother how he is.

   e) You say goodbye to a shopkeeper in a shop.

> *Buenas tardes*
> *Adiós*
> *Hasta luego*
> *¿Qué tal?*
> *Buenas noches*

3 Translate these phrases into English.

   a) Le presento a mi hermano.

   b) Esta es mi amiga.

   c) Encantado.

   d) Le presento a mi madre.

4 You are at your friend's house. Look at the sentences below and use "¿Puedo...?" ("May I...?") to ask if you can do these activities. Use the expressions in the box to help you.

> | | | |
> |---|---|---|
> | *escuchar música* | *comer galletas* | *ver la televisión* |
> | *poner la mesa* | *beber leche* | *jugar al fútbol* |

   a) May I eat biscuits?

   b) May I drink milk?

   c) May I watch television?

   d) May I lay the table?

   e) May I listen to music?

   f) May I play football?

Summary Questions

It's time for the best bit — loads of questions on the section you've just read. All the answers you need are in the section. If you're stuck, just look back at the relevant page to help you. It might look like a lot of questions, but they're really quick to do. Go through them and check your answers are right. If they're not, go back and do them again...

1) How do you say these numbers in Spanish?
   a) 13   b) 28   c) 39   d) 77   e) 100

2) How do you say 'third' in Spanish? (Give the masculine and feminine version.)

3) How do you say "What time is it?" in Spanish?

4) You ask a Mexican the time and he says "Son las tres y media". What time is it?

5) How do you say "It's twenty past four" in Spanish?

6) How would you say these times in Spanish?
   a) at ten o'clock   b) at ten to three   c) at half past one

7) You ask your friend Lola when she normally goes to the sports centre.
   She says "Voy los viernes". Which day does she go?

8) How do you say 'tomorrow' in Spanish? (Don't forget the accent.)

9) What is 'Sunday' in Spanish?

10) Write down the month you were born in Spanish.

11) You ask your friend when his birthday is, and he replies "El doce de agosto." When is it?

12) Write down today's date as if you were putting it in a letter.
    Don't forget to put where you're writing from, too.

13) How would you say hello in the following situations? (Don't use ¡Hola!)
    a) in the morning   b) at night   c) in the evening

14) Your friend Puri says "¡Hasta pronto!". What is she saying?

15) Your Spanish friend has just introduced you to their brother, Javier. How would
    you say "pleased to meet you" in Spanish? Write down two ways of saying this.

16) Your friend Miguel says "¿Qué tal?" Tell him in Spanish that you feel terrible.

17) You ask Miguel how he is and he says "Muy bien". What is he saying?

18) What are the Spanish words for "please" and "thank you".

19) How would you say "you're welcome" in Spanish?

20) Now Miguel is saying "Lo siento mucho". What does he mean?

21) You want to ask someone the way in Granada. How do you attract their attention?

22) How would you say "yes" and "no" in Spanish?

23) Write down "I would like a coffee" in Spanish.

24) How do you say "I would like to go to the cinema" in Spanish?

Your Details

Me, myself and I. My three favourite topics of conversation...

Talking about yourself — facts and figures

You need to know how to ask and answer these questions.
Change the highlighted words to answer about yourself.

①   *¿Cómo te llamas?*   = What are you called?

   Me llamo Lola.   = I'm called Lola.

②   *¿Cuántos años tienes?*   = How old are you?

   Tengo trece años.   = I'm thirteen.

> *See p.1 for more numbers and p.4 for more dates.*

③   *¿Cuándo es tu cumpleaños?*   = When is your birthday?

   Mi cumpleaños es el dos de abril.   = My birthday is the 2nd of April.

④   *¿Qué te gusta?*   = What do you like?

> *You can say anything you like here — sports (p.65), hobbies (p.67) or animals (p.17).*

   Me gusta el tenis.   = I like tennis.

This page has all the basics to start a conversation in Spanish

The stuff on this page is going to come up again and again while you're learning Spanish.
My advice to you is to learn it really well, right now, so it doesn't bother you later on.

Your Details

Learn how to say <u>what you look like</u>. But remember, beauty is only <u>skin deep</u>.

Say what you **look like**

Use this vocab for physical features such as <u>eyes</u>, <u>hair</u> and <u>body shape</u>.

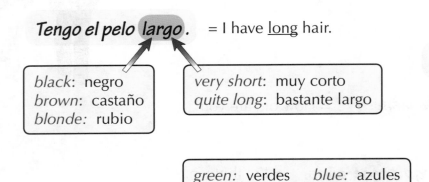

Soy alto/a. = I am <u>tall</u>.

slim: delgado/a   *medium height:* de talla mediana
fat: gordo/a   *short (in height):* bajo/a

Use the "-o" endings if you're a boy and the "-a" endings if you're a girl.

Tengo el pelo largo. = I have <u>long</u> hair.

black: negro
brown: castaño
blonde: rubio

very short: muy corto
quite long: bastante largo

Soy pelirrojo/a.

= I have red hair.

green: verdes   *blue:* azules

Tengo los ojos marrones. = I have <u>brown</u> eyes.

Llevo gafas. = I wear glasses.   **No llevo gafas.** = I don't wear glasses.

Describe your **personality**

Soy inteligente. = I am <u>intelligent</u>.

nice: simpático/a   *sporty:* deportista
shy: tímido/a   *hardworking:* trabajador(a)
lazy: perezoso/a

"Deportista" ends in an "a" for boys and girls. For "trabajador", you just add an "a" for girls.

Learn to describe yourself — inside and out

This is really useful vocab that you're going to need to describe yourself and other people.
Make sure you know it off by heart — cover it, test yourself and then test yourself again.

Your Family

You can choose your friends but you can't choose your family — just like you can't avoid this vocab at KS3. It's not so bad though — most pairs use the <u>same word</u> with <u>different endings</u>.

Use these words for your **friends** and **family**

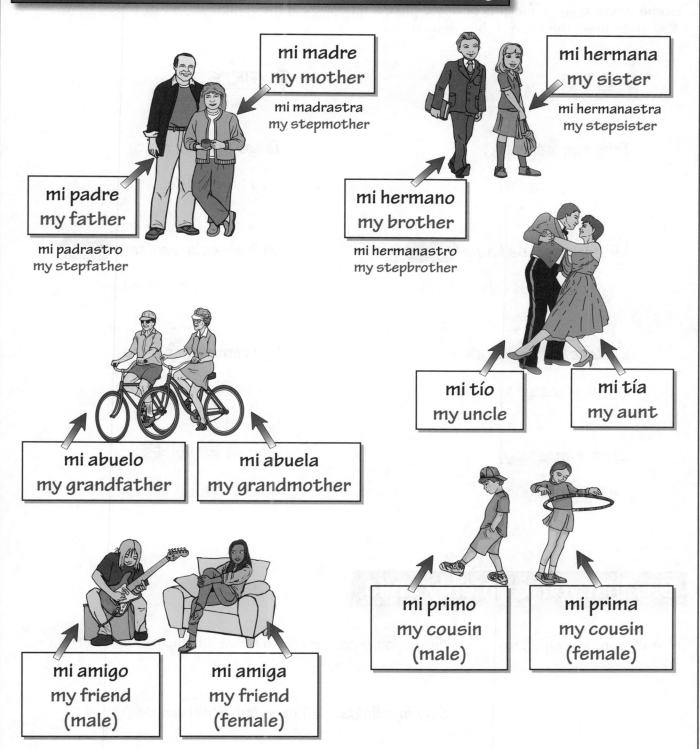

mi madre
my mother

mi madrastra
my stepmother

mi hermana
my sister

mi hermanastra
my stepsister

mi padre
my father

mi padrastro
my stepfather

mi hermano
my brother

mi hermanastro
my stepbrother

mi tío
my uncle

mi tía
my aunt

mi abuelo
my grandfather

mi abuela
my grandmother

mi primo
my cousin
(male)

mi prima
my cousin
(female)

mi amigo
my friend
(male)

mi amiga
my friend
(female)

Keep an eye on those "-o" or "-a" endings

It's easy to confuse masculine and feminine family names if you don't pay attention to the endings. It's a basic mistake that you want to avoid, so remember — o for a b<u>o</u>y, a for a g<u>a</u>l.

Your Family

You've learnt the Spanish names for family members — now learn to talk about them too.

Say what your family and friends are like

Some words change for girls or boys. Take a little look at the sentences below to see how.
I've underlined the Spanish bits that change.

⚉ BOYS

Tengo un hermano.

= I have a brother.

Mi hermano se llama David.

= My brother is called David.

Él tiene dieciséis años.

= He is sixteen years old.

Él es simpático.

= He is nice.

⚉ GIRLS

Tengo una hermana.

= I have a sister.

Mi hermana se llama Luisa.

= My sister is called Luisa.

Ella tiene diez años.

= She is ten years old.

Ella es simpática.

= She is nice.

Say that you're an only child

If you're an only child, say: *Soy hijo único.*   = I'm an only child (male).

Soy hija única.   = I'm an only child (female).

Being able to talk about people you know is really important at KS3

Even if you have a cart-load of siblings you need to know what "soy hijo/a único/a" means.
And if you're an only child, you could practise talking about a friend or another relative.

Pets and Animals

Animals are <u>much nicer</u> than people, except my sister's hamster, which bites.
Whether you've got pets or not, it's <u>useful</u> to know <u>animal names</u>.

Learn the animals — **Los animales**

Don't forget to learn if they go with "<u>un</u>" or "<u>una</u>".

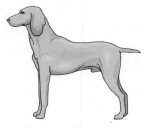

un perro
a dog

un conejo
a rabbit

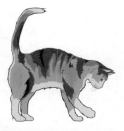

un gato
a cat

un hámster
a hamster

un ratón
a mouse

un pájaro
a bird

una tortuga
a tortoise

un caballo
a horse

Grab a dictionary if you have an unusual or exotic pet

These are the basic animals you need to know for KS3 — cover the labels and test yourself
until you know them all. If you have a more exciting pet, find out the vocab for that too.

Pets and Animals

Now you know <u>names for pets</u>, you can learn to <u>talk about them</u> too.

I have a cat — Tengo un gato

To talk about <u>your</u> pet, change "<u>gato</u>" in this example to match <u>your</u> animal.
Even if you don't have any pets, you need to <u>understand</u> what other people say about theirs.

¿Tienes animales en casa?   = Do you have any pets?

You can also ask "¿Tienes mascotas?"

Tengo un gato.   = I have <u>a cat</u>.

Mi gato se llama Alfie.   = <u>My cat</u> is called Alfie.

Mi gato es simpático.   = <u>My cat</u> is <u>nice</u>.

Remember, the "o" endings go with "un" animals, and the "a" endings go with "una" animals.

fat:	gordo/a
black:	negro/a
pretty:	bonito/a
ugly:	feo/a

See p.60 for more colours. For other adjectives, check a dictionary.

Learn what to say if you **don't have pets**

Even if you have loads of pets, you <u>need to know</u> what this phrase means.

No tengo animales en casa.   = I don't have any pets.

Learn this vocab and impress Spanish animal lovers

Don't just learn the word for your pet. Learn a range of adjectives so you can describe your pet and understand what people say about theirs. It might be useful if you go on an exchange.

Practice Questions

Track 3   Listening Question

1   Listen to Elena talking about her family and pets.
     Write each name next to who they are in the family.

Mother	Enrique
Stepfather	Fernando
Sister	Félix
Brother	Alicia
Aunt	Inés
Cousin	Pablo
Dog	Juana
Cat	Max

2   Write sentences in Spanish describing yourself as if you were these people.
     For example: Michael — tall, green eyes, short hair.

   Me llamo Michael. Soy alto. Tengo los ojos verdes y el pelo corto.

   a)   Jasmine — short, brown eyes, blonde hair.

   b)   David — blue eyes, black hair, wears glasses.

   c)   Sophie — medium height, slim, long hair.

   d)   Gareth — fat, red hair, doesn't wear glasses.

   Make sure you use a verb and try to link some of the details with "y" (and).

3   Write down the English for these animals.

   a)   un perro   c)   un pájaro

   b)   un caballo   d)   un ratón

Your Home

Most people spend a fair bit of time <u>at home</u> — that's why you need this vocab.

Talk about the rooms in your house — Las habitaciones

el salón
living room

el comedor
dining room

la cocina
kitchen

el dormitorio
bedroom

el cuarto de baño
bathroom

el jardín
garden

In my house — En mi casa

Remember, "<u>mi casa</u>" means "my house" and "<u>tu casa</u>" means "your house".

¿Qué hay en tu casa? = What is there in your house?

Change the bits in the green boxes to make sentences about your own home.

En mi casa hay cinco habitaciones.

= In my house there are <u>five</u> rooms.

En mi casa hay un salón, una cocina y dos dormitorios.

= In my house there is <u>a living room, a kitchen and two bedrooms</u>.

Home sweet home — learn to show it off in Spanish

Your house and where you live is a key topic at KS3, so it's important to get to grips with it.
Make up a few sentences to explain what's in your house, or your dream house if you'd rather.

Your Home

Okay, so this is far from the most exciting vocab you're ever going to learn. Unfortunately, it's part of KS3 <u>vocab about the home</u>, so there's no escaping it.

Talk about the furniture — **Los muebles**

Think of it this way — a home wouldn't be a home without <u>furniture</u>.

un sillón
armchair

un sofá
sofa

una cama
bed

una mesa
table

un armario
wardrobe

una silla
chair

In your room — **En tu dormitorio**

Remember that to say "<u>a</u>" in Spanish, "<u>el</u>" changes to "<u>un</u>" and "<u>la</u>" changes to "<u>una</u>".

¿Qué hay en tu dormitorio?   = What is there in your bedroom?

Hay una cama, un armario y una mesa.   = There is <u>a bed, a wardrobe and a table</u>.

As always, remember to learn whether the words use "un" or "una"

If you do a Spanish exchange, this kind of vocab could be surprisingly useful. People might tell you where to leave things, where to put things or where you'll be sleeping.

Where You Live

There's no place like home, and this page will teach you to say where it is.

Where do you live? — ¿Dónde vives?

1) Learn the names of <u>types of home</u>:

Vivo en...

= I live in...

una casa
a house

un apartamento
a flat

una granja
a farm

2) And learn the words for <u>where you live</u>:

Vivo en...

= I live in...

un pueblo
a village

una ciudad
a town / city

Some extra sentences

Use these <u>sentences</u> to give <u>more detail</u> on where you live.

Vivo en el campo. = I live in the countryside.

Vivo en las montañas. = I live in the mountains.

Vivo cerca del mar. = I live near the sea.

Cover up the labels for these eight pictures and test yourself

You can bet your boots that if you start chatting to a Spanish person in Spanish, one of the first things they'll ask you is where you live. So this vocab is definitely worth remembering.

Where You Live

As this page will show you, there's <u>plenty more</u> you can say about where you live.

Say **exactly** where you live

Change the <u>highlighted bits</u> in this example sentence so it's about where <u>you</u> live.
Then learn your sentence <u>off by heart</u> — trust me, you'll be using it <u>a lot</u>.

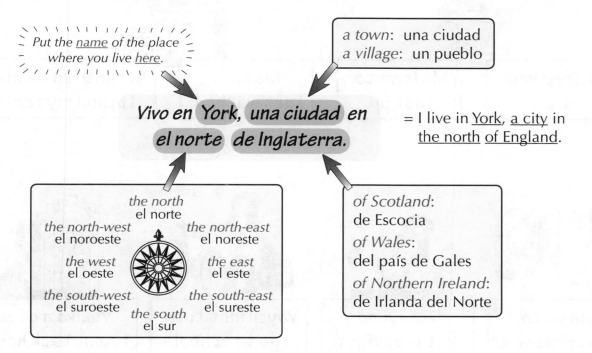

Put the <u>name</u> of the place where you live <u>here</u>.

a town: una ciudad
a village: un pueblo

Vivo en York, una ciudad en el norte de Inglaterra.

= I live in <u>York</u>, <u>a city</u> in <u>the north</u> <u>of England</u>.

the north
el norte

the north-west
el noroeste

the north-east
el noreste

the west
el oeste

the east
el este

the south-west
el suroeste

the south-east
el sureste

the south
el sur

of Scotland:
de Escocia

of Wales:
del país de Gales

of Northern Ireland:
de Irlanda del Norte

Do you like living here? — ¿Te gusta vivir aquí?

Giving <u>opinions</u> is the key to <u>doing well</u> in Spanish — and it'll make you sound <u>more interesting</u>.

Me gusta vivir aquí...

= I like living here...

...porque es tranquilo.

= ...because it is <u>peaceful</u>.

clean: limpio
great: estupendo

No me gusta vivir aquí...

= I don't like living here...

...porque es aburrido.

= ...because it is <u>boring</u>.

dirty: sucio
horrible: horrible

The more details you can give, the better

Really short answers can sound a bit dull and sulky. Always try to say as much as you can when you're asked a question and if you can, give an opinion. I know you've got one.

Daily Routine

You might find this a bit... <u>routine</u>. But I bet you this kind of vocab will come in handy.

Daily routine — **Say what you do**

"Me" + a verb usually means the verb is <u>reflexive</u>. See p.128-129 for an explanation.

Me despierto. I wake up.	**Me levanto.** I get up.	**Me lavo.** I get washed.	**Me lavo los dientes.** I brush my teeth.

See p.75 for methods of transport.

Me visto. I get dressed.	**Desayuno.** I eat breakfast.	**Voy al instituto.** I go to school.	**Vuelvo a casa.** I come back home.

Hago mis deberes. I do my homework.	**Veo la televisión.** I watch TV.	**Ceno.** I eat dinner.	**Me acuesto.** I go to bed.

If you can add in the <u>time of day</u> you do something, that sounds really good:

Me levanto a las siete. = I get up at <u>seven o'clock</u>.

See p.2 for how to tell the time.

You guessed it — cover up those labels and test yourself

For KS3, you pretty much have to know your daily routine inside out and back to front. Write out your own daily routine, including the times you do everything, and learn it off by heart.

Chores

Here's a bunch of <u>chores</u> that you might have to do at home. If you <u>don't</u> do any chores at home — lucky you. But you still need to <u>learn</u> them for KS3 Spanish.

Learn this vocab for **helping at home**

¿Ayudas en casa? = Do you help at home?

Paso la aspiradora. = I do the vacuum cleaning.

Arreglo mi dormitorio. = I tidy my room.

Lavo los platos. = I wash the dishes.

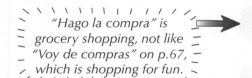

Limpio la casa. = I clean the house.

"Hago la compra" is grocery shopping, not like "Voy de compras" on p.67, which is shopping for fun. → *Hago la compra.* = I do the shopping.

Pongo la mesa. = I lay the table.

Hago mi cama. = I make my bed.

Lavo el coche. = I clean the car.

Learn what to say if you **don't help at home**

No hago nada. = I don't do anything.

Learning Spanish — always a pleasure, never a chore

Cover up the English and test yourself on these chores. Then check your answers and do it again until you get them all right. About as much fun as making your bed, but more useful.

Practice Questions

<u>Listening Questions</u>

1   Listen to these people (a-d) talking about where they live.
    Write down whether each statement is true or false.

    a)   Esteban's city, Segovia, is in the north-west of Spain.

    b)   The village where Beatriz lives is very boring.

    c)   The village where Alfonso lives is near the sea.

    d)   Leticia likes where she lives because it is fun.

Track 5

    Listen to Miguel and Isabel describing their daily routine.
    Write down whether each statement is true or false.

2   a)   Miguel gets up at 6.30.

    b)   Miguel does his homework after he eats his dinner.

    c)   Miguel goes to bed at 10 o'clock.

3   a)   Isabel has a wash at 6.45.

    b)   Isabel has breakfast at 8.30.

    c)   Isabel watches TV at 9 o'clock.

4   These Spanish words for rooms in a house have all been misspelt.
    Unscramble the letters and write the correct names for each room in Spanish.

    a)   le urtoca ed oñba   c)   le andríj   e)   al incaco

    b)   le oriomordit   d)   le rocomed   f)   le lasnó

5   Write down the Spanish for these items of furniture. Don't forget 'un' or 'una'.

    a)   a table   c)   a bed   e)   a wardrobe

    b)   a sofa   d)   a chair   f)   an armchair

6   Write down the Spanish for the following words.

    a)   a flat   b)   a house   c)   a village   d)   a city

Practice Questions

7   Write out in Spanish what each person is saying about where they live.

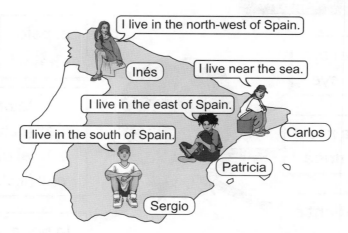

8   Write out these sentences in Spanish.

a)   I have dinner.

b)   I have breakfast.

c)   I get up.

d)   I wake up.

e)   I get dressed.

f)   I go to bed.

9   Copy and complete these sentences, using the verbs from the box.

a)   ……… los platos.

b)   ……… la aspiradora.

c)   ……… mi dormitorio.

d)   ……… mi cama.

e)   ……… la mesa.

lavo	*hago*	*paso*
pongo	*arreglo*	

10   Write out in Spanish what these people say about their chores. For example:

Jake: On Sundays I wash the car.   *Los domingos lavo el coche.*

a)   **Sarah**: On Mondays I make my bed and I tidy my bedroom.

b)   **Richard**: On Tuesdays I do the vacuuming and I do the shopping.

c)   **Louise**: I lay the table and I wash the dishes.

d)   **Paul**: I don't do anything. I am very lazy.

The Body

Body parts are really <u>useful</u>, especially if you're <u>ill</u> or if you <u>hurt something</u> (see p.30).

The head — La cabeza

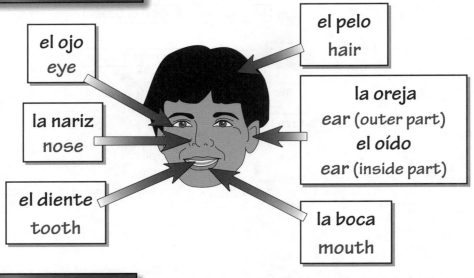

el ojo
eye

la nariz
nose

el diente
tooth

el pelo
hair

la oreja
ear (outer part)
el oído
ear (inside part)

la boca
mouth

The body — El cuerpo

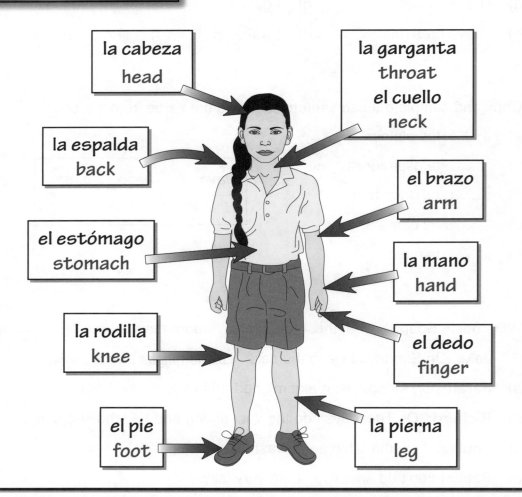

la cabeza
head

la espalda
back

el estómago
stomach

la rodilla
knee

el pie
foot

la garganta
throat
el cuello
neck

el brazo
arm

la mano
hand

el dedo
finger

la pierna
leg

No complex grammar here — just good, old-fashioned vocab

This page is simply begging you to cover the labels and test yourself on the vocab. Keep testing yourself until you get them all right, then give yourself a pat on the "espalda".

Health and Illness

It's horrible when you feel ill, and even worse if you're supposed to be on holiday.
At least with this handy vocab, you could get a Spanish doctor to fix you up ASAP.

Tell someone you're ill — Estoy enfermo/a

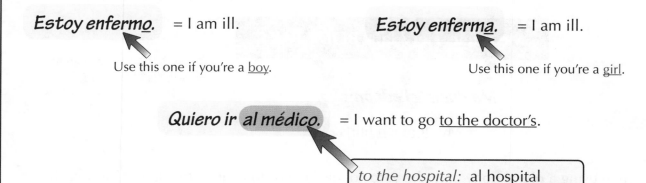

Estoy enfermo. = I am ill.

Use this one if you're a boy.

Estoy enferma. = I am ill.

Use this one if you're a girl.

Quiero ir al médico. = I want to go to the doctor's.

to the hospital: al hospital
to the pharmacy: a la farmacia

Learn these things for **making you better**

If you feel ill, this is the kind of stuff you might need.

una tirita
a plaster

una crema
a cream

unas pastillas
some tablets

un jarabe
a syrup

una receta
a prescription

Here's how to ask for something: *Necesito una tirita.* = I need a plaster.

It's not being paranoid to learn this page

Even if you never need this vocab in a real life situation, you're definitely going to come across it in KS3 Spanish exercises. So unless you want a big fat zero as your mark, learn this page.

Health and Illness

I told you that body vocab on p.28 would come in handy...

My arm hurts — Me duele el brazo

1) It's important that you can explain what hurts, especially if you're at the doctor's (p.29).

Me duele + el / la + BODY PART

Me duele **el estómago.**

= My stomach hurts.

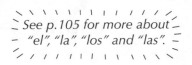

See p.105 for more about "el", "la", "los" and "las".

2) If you're using a plural body part, the verb "duele" needs to change to "duelen" to match:

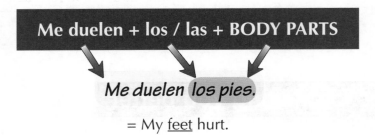

Me duelen + los / las + BODY PARTS

Me duelen **los pies.**

= My feet hurt.

You can use this sentence for any body part

Me duele **el cuello.**

= My neck hurts.

Me duele **la cabeza.**

= My head hurts. (I have a headache).

Me duele **la espalda.**

= My back hurts.

"Piernas" is plural, so you use "duelen".

Me duelen **las piernas.**

= My legs hurt.

And here's one more useful sentence: **Tengo gripe.**   = I've got flu.

In Spanish you don't use "my" with body parts that hurt

In Spanish, you don't say "my legs hurt". Instead you say "the legs hurt". Never say "me duelen mis piernas" because that would be wrong. It's the same for every other body part.

Practice Questions

Track 6   <u>Listening Question</u>

1   Marc, Daniela and Carlos all feel ill. Listen to them talking about
     their problems and answer the questions below in English.

     a)   What illness does Marc think he has?

     b)   In addition to her legs, which two other parts of Daniela's body hurt?

     c)   Where does Daniela want to go?

     d)   What two things does Carlos say he needs?

     e)   Where does Carlos say he is going?

2   Write the Spanish for these words: a) the head   b) the body

3   Write out the body parts marked on the diagram in Spanish.

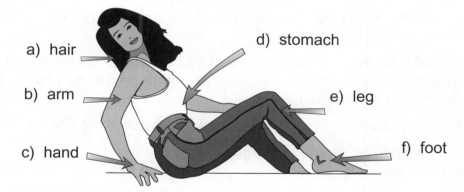

a) hair

b) arm

c) hand

d) stomach

e) leg

f) foot

4   Write down the Spanish for these items that you might buy from the pharmacy.

     a) some tablets   b) a plaster   c) a cream   d) a syrup

5   Copy and complete these sentences using 'me duele' or 'me duelen'.

     a) .... la garganta.   d) .... el estómago.

     b) .... los ojos.   e) .... la cabeza.

     c) .... los oídos.   f) .... los pies.

Summary Questions

There was quite a lot of different stuff in that section — personal info, family stuff, where you live, parts of the body, etc. To check that you've actually absorbed it all, it's time for some questions covering everything in the section. Answer the questions, correct the mistakes and answer them again until you get them all right.

1) How would you ask me what my name is in Spanish?

2) Answer these questions in Spanish:
a) ¿Cuántos años tienes?   b) ¿Cuándo es tu cumpleaños?

3) Describe what you look like in Spanish. Mention at least four things.

4) What do these words mean in English? a) tímido   b) perezoso   c) simpático

5) Write these words in Spanish:
a) my grandmother   b) my brother   c) my uncle   d) my cousin (female)

6) Write these sentences in Spanish:
"I have a sister. She has blonde hair. She is hardworking."

7) In Spanish, how do you ask someone if they have any pets?

8) What are these animals in Spanish?
a) a mouse   b) a tortoise   c) a cat   d) a rabbit   e) a hamster

9) Write down what these words mean in English:
a) el cuarto de baño   b) la cocina   c) el comedor   d) el jardín

10) In Spanish, answer the question "¿Qué hay en tu dormitorio?"
Mention at least three things.

11) Río and Luis live in the same town. Río likes living there because it's clean.
Luis doesn't like living there because it's boring. Write out what they would say about their town in Spanish.

12) Write in Spanish: "I live in Dover, a town in the south-east of England."

13) Write what these mean in English:
a) Desayuno.   b) Me acuesto.   c) Hago mis deberes.   d) Me levanto.

14) Write out your personal daily routine, including the time you do things.

15) How do you ask someone if they help at home in Spanish?

16) List five chores that you might do to help at home.

17) In Spanish, write labels for the diagram labelled a-g.

18) Andreas says "Me duele la espalda." What's wrong with him?

19) List three things in Spanish that you might buy from the pharmacy if you're unwell.

20) How would you tell a Spanish person that you're ill and want to go to the doctor's?

School Subjects

Learn to say the <u>subjects</u> in Spanish and then on p.34, you can say why you like (or hate) them.

School subjects — Las asignaturas

<u>Subjects</u> are really important so learn <u>all</u> of them — even those you <u>don't</u> study.

SCIENCE
las ciencias: science
la física: physics
la química: chemistry
la biología: biology

LANGUAGES
el francés: French
el alemán: German
el español: Spanish
el inglés: English

PHYSICAL EDUCATION
la educación física: PE

HUMANITIES
la historia: history
la geografía: geography
la religión: religious studies

ART AND MUSIC
el dibujo: art
la música: music

NUMBERS AND STUFF
las matemáticas: maths
la informática: IT

Say what you study

This is how you say <u>what you study</u> (just replace "español" with any of the subjects above):

Estudio + SUBJECT

Estudio **español.** = I study <u>Spanish</u>.

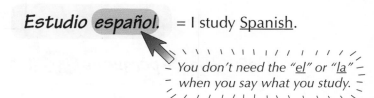

You don't need the "<u>el</u>" or "<u>la</u>" when you say what you study.

Educate yourself and learn all the subjects

There are quite a few subjects to learn on this page but they're all important. Learn them in groups (it might make them easier to remember) and then practise saying what you study.

School Subjects

Now it's time to give your <u>opinions</u> on the <u>subjects</u> you study. Be nice.

My favourite subject — Mi asignatura preferida

Tell everyone what your <u>favourite subject</u> is using this phrase:

Mi asignatura preferida es + SUBJECT

Mi asignatura preferida es la geografía. = My favourite subject is <u>geography</u>.

To say which <u>subjects</u> you <u>like</u>, you'd say:

Me gusta la biología. = I like <u>biology</u>.

When you talk about a subject that's <u>plural</u>, like science, "<u>me gusta</u>" changes to "<u>me gustan</u>".

Me gustan las ciencias. = I like <u>science</u>.

If you really <u>don't like a subject</u>, here's how to say it:

Odio la historia. = I hate <u>history</u>.   **Odio** las matemáticas. = I hate <u>maths</u>.

Give a reason for your choice

Always remember to say <u>why</u> you <u>do</u> or <u>don't like</u> it.

Me gusta el inglés **porque es** útil = I like <u>English</u> because it's <u>useful</u>.

> *interesting:* interesante
> *easy:* fácil

> *useless:* inútil
> *boring:* aburrido/a

Odio la física **porque es** difícil = I hate <u>physics</u> because it's <u>difficult</u>.

Nobody will believe you if you say you like all the subjects

Learn how to give your opinion — it's a really good habit to get into. If you give more details in an answer, your teacher probably won't ask you as many questions about your subjects.

School Routine

You spend enough time at school so you must know your school routine off by heart by now. This page is about getting to school and what you do when you get there.

The school day — La jornada escolar

Learn these phrases and change them to match your own school routine.

Me levanto a las siete. = I get up at 7:00.

For more on daily routine, see p.24.

Voy al instituto en coche. = I go to school by car.

For more on transport, see p.75.

on foot: a pie
by bus: en autobús
by bike: en bicicleta

Las clases empiezan a las nueve. = Lessons start at 9:00.

For more on time, see p.2.

Las clases terminan a las tres y media. = Lessons end at 3:30.

Cada clase dura cuarenta minutos. = Each lesson lasts 40 minutes.

Tenemos ocho clases por día. = We have 8 lessons per day.

For more on numbers, see p.1.

Hacemos una hora de deberes por día. = We do one hour of homework per day.

School, school and more school

It's always useful to be able to talk about your school day — teachers love to ask questions about what time you do certain things. Here's the chance to tell them about your routine.

Classroom Stuff

Spanish teachers really like to <u>talk</u> in <u>Spanish</u> — this page will help you <u>understand</u> them.

Sit down! — ¡Siéntate!

Make sure you know whether your <u>Spanish teacher</u> is telling you to "<u>sit down!</u>" or "<u>stand up!</u>"

Sit down = *¡Siéntate!*

For talking to <u>one person</u>.

Stand up = *¡Levántate!*

¡Sentaos!

For talking to <u>more than one person</u>.

¡Levantaos!

Commands for one person are different to commands for more than one person. See p.135-136 for more info.

And when they want you to <u>be quiet</u>: *¡Silencio!* = Silence!

Use these phrases if you're stuck

If you <u>don't know</u> how to say something, <u>ask in Spanish</u> what it <u>means</u>:

¿Qué quiere decir eso? = What does that mean?

For more on how to ask questions, see p.101-102.

¿Cómo se dice en español? = How do you say it <u>in Spanish</u>?

¿Cómo se dice en inglés? = How do you say it <u>in English</u>?

True or false?

Verdadero = True   *Falso* = False

Stay out of trouble and learn this page

You'll earn double brownie points from your teacher if you speak in Spanish in the classroom.
If you don't know how to say something in Spanish, use "¿Cómo se dice en español?".

Classroom Stuff

If your teacher asks you to take your "<u>libro</u>" and "<u>cuaderno</u>" out, you'll need this vocab.

In the classroom — **En el aula**

If you need a <u>pen</u>, you say, "<u>Quisiera un bolígrafo, por favor</u>" (I'd like a pen, please).

un bolígrafo
pen

un lápiz
pencil

una regla
ruler

un libro
book

una *goma*
rubber

un uniforme
uniform

un horario
timetable

un *cuaderno*
exercise book

More **school** words

una *clase*
lesson

un alumno (boy)
una alumna (girl)
pupil

un aula
classroom

un *profesor* (man)
una *profesora* (woman)
teacher

These change for <u>male</u> and <u>female</u> versions.

You'll hear these words all the time in the classroom

Learn all this vocab and impress your teacher by asking them for classroom things in Spanish. You can change "<u>un bolígrafo</u>" in "quisiera <u>un bolígrafo</u>" for any item, like "un cuaderno".

Practice Questions

Track 7

Listening Question

1 Listen to Pedro giving his opinions on his school subjects. Copy out the table and put a tick in the correct column to show which subjects Pedro likes and dislikes. The first one has been done for you.

Subject	Like	Dislike
Maths		✓
Geography		
Chemistry		
German		
Art		
History		

2 Write down the Spanish names for these subjects.

a) history

b) physics

c) German

d) biology

e) PE

f) IT

g) French

h) science

i) religious studies

3 Copy and complete these sentences by translating the bits in brackets into Spanish.

a) *[I get up]* a las ocho.

b) Las clases *[start]* a las nueve.

c) Las clases *[end]* a las cuatro y media.

d) *[We have]* ocho clases por día.

e) *[We do]* una hora de deberes por día.

4 Copy these words and write '**un**' for masculine words and '**una**' for feminine words in the gaps. Then translate all the words into English.

a) ....*un*.... libro = *book*

b) .... profesora

c) .... cuaderno

d) .... horario

e) .... clase

f) .... regla

Jobs

In Spanish, the word for a job can depend on <u>who's doing it</u>. The 🧍 words are for <u>men</u> and the 🧍 words are for <u>women</u>. 🧍🧍 means it's the same word for <u>both men and women</u>.

Lots of jobs — Muchos trabajos [el trabajo = job]

🧍🧍 el/la dentista
dentist

🧍 el médico
🧍 la médica
doctor

🧍 el enfermero
🧍 la enfermera
nurse

🧍 el peluquero
🧍 la peluquera
hairdresser

🧍🧍 el/la albañil
builder

🧍 el ingeniero
🧍 la ingeniera
engineer

🧍 el mecánico
🧍 la mecánica
mechanic

🧍🧍 el/la policía
police officer

🧍 el vendedor
🧍 la vendedora
salesperson

🧍 el profesor
🧍 la profesora
teacher

🧍 el actor
🧍 la actriz
actor

🧍 el secretario
🧍 la secretaria
secretary

Revising KS3 Spanish — it's all work, work, work

This job vocab is really useful for talking about what your family does. Don't forget to learn the male and female versions too. You can put all this into practice on the next page.

Talking about Jobs

Use the jobs from p.39 to say what your family does. If the job you're looking for isn't on p.39, look it up in the <u>dictionary</u>.

Say what **you** and **other people do**

If you've got a job, learn to say <u>what you do</u>. Learn how to say what <u>your parents do</u> too.

Soy + JOB

Soy **dentista.** = I'm a <u>dentist</u>.

Mi padre es **mecánico.** = My father is a <u>mechanic</u>.

Don't forget to use the <u>correct masculine</u> or <u>feminine</u> version of the job.

Remember, you don't need "un" or "una" when you're talking about which jobs people do.

Mi madre es **profesora.** = My mother is a <u>teacher</u>.

I work part-time — **Trabajo a tiempo parcial**

If you're doing <u>KS3 Spanish</u>, you <u>probably won't</u> have a <u>full-time job</u> yet. Here's how to say that you're a <u>student</u> or that you have a <u>part-time job</u>.

Soy estudiante. = I am a student.

Trabajo a tiempo parcial. = I work part-time.

Trabajo en '*Pets R us*'. = I work at '<u>Pets R us</u>'.

Reparto periódicos. = I deliver newspapers.

If you don't have a job, learn how to say that you're a student

You've got two options here — you can either say what you and your family do or where you work. And for double points, you need to be able to say both. It's not rocket science.

Talking about Jobs

You might not know <u>what you want to study</u> or <u>what you want to be</u> when you leave school. If you don't know, <u>make something up</u> — don't just say "I don't know".

Say what you want to study — **Quiero estudiar...**

This is how to say what you want to <u>study</u> (for GCSEs or A-levels):

> ### Quiero estudiar + SUBJECT

For more on subjects, see p.33.

> *Quiero estudiar* biología*...*   = I want to study <u>biology</u>...

Don't forget to give a <u>reason</u>:   *...porque* es útil*.*   = ...because <u>it's useful</u>.

> *it's interesting:* es interesante
> *it's easy:* es fácil
> *it's fun:* es divertido/a

> *Quiero estudiar* español *porque* es interesante   = I want to study <u>Spanish</u> because <u>it's interesting</u>.

Say what you want to be — **Quiero ser...**

Say what you want to <u>be</u> like this:

> ### Quiero ser + JOB

Quiero ser actor*.* = I want to be an <u>actor</u>.

Give a <u>reason</u> — you can use the reasons above, or this one's good too:

> *Quiero ser* médico *porque* ganan mucho dinero   = I want to be a <u>doctor</u> because <u>they earn a lot of money</u>.

I want to be rich and famous

Teachers love asking questions about the future so make sure you know how to reply to them if they ask. Don't forget that a reason to back up your answer will be even more impressive.

Practice Questions

Track 8 <u>Listening Questions</u>

Enrique and María are talking about which jobs their family members do. Listen to what they say and answer the questions below in English.

1 a) What job does Enrique's father do?

b) Which member of Enrique's family is a hairdresser?

c) What job does Enrique want to do when he is older?

2 a) What job does María's mother do?

b) What job does María's uncle do?

c) Which member of María's family is an actress?

3 Write the correct number next to each letter to match the Spanish words on the left to their English meanings on the right.

a) el secretario   **1** mechanic

b) el policía   **2** builder

c) el mecánico   **3** nurse

d) el ingeniero   **4** secretary

e) la enfermera   **5** engineer

f) la vendedora   **6** saleswoman

g) el albañil   **7** police officer

4 Rearrange the words so that these sentences make sense, then write out the full sentences in Spanish. Use the English translation to help you.

a) ser médico quiero porque útil es
[I want to be a doctor because it's useful.]

b) dentista quiero es porque interesante ser
[I want to be a dentist because it's interesting.]

c) estudiar porque inglés quiero fácil es
[I want to study English because it's easy.]

d) ganan ingeniero quiero ser mucho porque dinero
[I want to be an engineer because they earn a lot of money.]

e) estudiar quiero dibujo divertido es porque
[I want to study art because it's fun.]

Summary Questions

I've got some good news and some bad news. The bad news is, you've got a page of questions to do. The good news is, you'll have earned yourself a cup of tea by the end of it. And if you get them all right first time round, I'd say you deserve a choccy biscuit too. Answer all of these questions — look up any answers you don't know and then try again.

1) Write a sentence in Spanish for each subject you study, starting with 'Estudio'.

2) Which subjects do you like? Which do you hate?
Answer in Spanish, in full sentences, and don't forget to give a reason for each one.

3) In Spanish, write down how you get to school.

4) How do you say that you have six lessons per day?

5) How long is each lesson at your school? Write it down in Spanish
— make sure you write the number out in full too.

6) Write down in Spanish that you do two hours of homework per day.

7) If you hear your teacher shouting these, what are they telling you to do?
a) ¡Sentaos!   b) ¡Silencio!   c) ¡Levantaos!

8) Write down how to say 'true' and 'false' in Spanish.

9) Your teacher points at a pen and says "¿Cómo se dice en español?".
What would you say?

10) Your teacher just loves speaking Spanish. She says:
"¿Cómo se dice "un cuaderno" en inglés?". What would your answer be?

11) Write down the names in Spanish for:
a) a pencil   b) a ruler   c) a timetable   d) a uniform

12) What are these in English?
a) un profesor   b) un libro   c) una goma   d) un alumno

13) What are these jobs in Spanish?
(Give the male and female versions, including 'el' and 'la'.)
a) doctor   b) teacher   c) hairdresser   d) nurse   e) actor

14) Write down what job you want to do. Say what jobs your parents do too.

15) How would you say that you work part-time at 'RapidBurgerz'?

16) Write in Spanish:
"I want to study IT because it's useful."
"I want to be an engineer because it's interesting."

17) What does this mean? "Quiero estudiar español porque es divertido."

18) Write down this sentence in Spanish: "I want to be a salesperson because it's easy."

Directions

It's <u>dead important</u> to learn to ask for directions for <u>KS3 Spanish</u>.
It's also really <u>useful</u> if you're <u>lost</u> in a <u>Spanish-speaking country</u>.

Where is... ? — ¿Dónde está... ?

There are <u>two</u> questions you can ask to <u>find your way</u> somewhere — you need to know <u>both</u> of them.

(1) *¿Dónde está la estación?* = Where is <u>the station</u>?

> Replace the bits in green boxes with any place from p.47.

(2) *¿Para ir al banco?* = How do I get <u>to the bank</u>?

Use "<u>al</u>" for "<u>el</u>" words and "<u>a la</u>" for "<u>la</u>" words — they both mean "<u>to the</u>".

¿Para ir a la piscina? = How do I get <u>to the swimming pool</u>?

Distances — ask if it's near or far

If the place you're looking for is <u>miles away</u>, you don't just want to set off walking there.
Here's the <u>question</u> you need to ask:

¿Está lejos de aquí? = Is it far from here?

Here are some <u>answers</u> you might hear:

Está lejos. = It's <u>far away</u>.   *Está cerca.* = It's <u>nearby</u>.

Está a dos kilómetros. = It's <u>two</u> kilometres away.

This can be replaced with any number — see p.1.

Get out of a pickle if you're lost in Spain

You might think learning this stuff in class is boring, but believe me, when you're lost, trying to find 'La Rambla' in Barcelona, with only Spaniards around, you'll be more than grateful for it.

Directions

The previous page was about asking someone for <u>directions</u> but it's <u>pretty useless</u> if you <u>don't understand</u> the reply. Here's how to understand <u>directions in Spanish</u>.

You'll need to **understand directions**

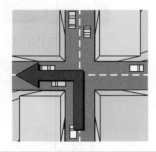

Gire a la izquierda
Turn left

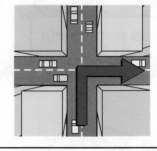

Gire a la derecha
Turn right

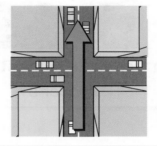

Siga todo recto
Go straight on

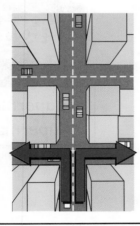

Tome la primera calle a
la izquierda / derecha
Take the first road on
the left / right

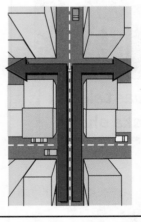

Tome la segunda calle a
la izquierda / derecha
Take the second road on
the left / right

Left is "la izquierda" and right is "la derecha"

If a Spanish person tells you how to get to the station, you'll be glad you learnt this page.
Make sure you don't confuse "derecha" and "izquierda" and you'll be able to get anywhere.

Shops

Learn the names of these <u>shops</u> that you might want to visit.

la panadería
baker's

la carnicería
butcher's

la farmacia
pharmacy

la confitería
sweet shop

la tienda de comestibles
grocer's

el quiosco
newsagent's

la pastelería
cake shop

el mercado
market

el supermercado
supermarket

el banco
bank

It's easy to get these two <u>mixed up</u> — "<u>la librería</u>" means <u>bookshop</u> and "<u>la biblioteca</u>" means <u>library</u>.

la librería
bookshop

la biblioteca
library

Learn this vocab so you can go shopping in Spain

This shopping vocab isn't too tricky — just eleven names to remember (alright, twelve if you count "library"). Don't forget to make sure you learn whether they're masculine or feminine.

Places in Town

These <u>places</u> will come in useful if you visit any <u>Spanish town</u>.

el parque
park

el teatro
theatre

Correos
post office

la iglesia
church

"Correos" is <u>masculine</u> but it's not used with the article — it just <u>stays as</u> "<u>Correos</u>".

el cine
cinema

la piscina
swimming pool

el polideportivo
leisure centre

el museo
museum

el castillo
castle

el hospital
hospital

el hotel
hotel

la estación (de trenes)
railway station

la oficina de turismo
tourist office

el ayuntamiento
town hall

Touristy vocab — just in case you want to be a Spanish tour guide
Your teacher might ask you what you did on holiday and if you don't know how to say you went to the castle, it might get a bit awkward. That means you need to learn all these places.

Practice Questions

<u>Listening Question</u>

1   Listen to three people (a-c) asking for directions. Starting from X each time, follow each set of directions and write down the number of the place each person is directed to.

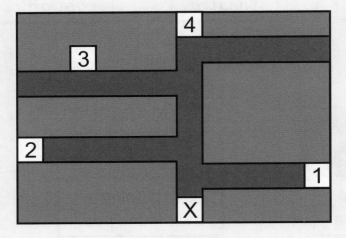

2   Translate these sentences into English.

a)   ¿Está lejos de aquí?

b)   Está a tres kilómetros.

c)   Está cerca.

d)   Está lejos.

3   Where would you go to do the following things? Write a Spanish shop from the box for each one.

a)   Buy some tomatoes for a salad.

b)   Change some pounds into euros.

c)   Buy some cream for your insect bites.

d)   Buy some meat for your barbecue.

e)   Buy a Spanish to English dictionary.

f)   Buy a cream cake.

> *la pastelería*
> *la tienda de comestibles*
> *la farmacia*
> *la librería*
> *la carnicería*
> *el banco*

4   Write these sentences about places in town in Spanish.

a)   In my town, there's a castle.

b)   There's a town hall and a church.

c)   There's a museum and a park.

d)   There's no swimming pool.

e)   There's no station in my town.

f)   There's a cinema and a theatre.

Fruit and Vegetables

A page of <u>healthiness</u> — learn all of these <u>fruits</u> and <u>vegetables</u>.

Fruit — Las frutas   ["la fruta" = fruit]

el plátano
banana

la naranja
orange

la manzana
apple

el melocotón
peach

la pera
pear

el limón
lemon

la fresa
strawberry

Vegetables — Las verduras   ["la verdura" = vegetable]

la patata
potato

la cebolla
onion

el champiñón
mushroom

la coliflor
cauliflower

las judías
beans

los guisantes
peas

la zanahoria
carrot

el tomate
tomato

la lechuga
lettuce

Even if you don't like cauliflower, you still need to know how to say it

You'll have no problems in a greengrocer's if you learn this whole page off by heart. It'll also help if your Spanish teacher wants to do supermarket role plays or talk about favourite foods.

Meat and Other Food

Here are just about all the <u>meats</u> and <u>carbs</u> you'll need to know how to say in Spanish.

Meat — La carne

| la *carne de vaca* |
| beef |

| la *carne de cerdo* |
| pork |

| el *cordero* |
| lamb |

| el *pollo* |
| chicken |

| el *jamón* |
| ham |

| el *filete* |
| steak |

| la *hamburguesa* |
| burger |

| la *salchicha* |
| sausage |

| el *pescado* |
| fish |

| los *mariscos* |
| seafood/shellfish |

Other Tasty Stuff

| el *pan* |
| bread |

| los *cereales* |
| cereal |

| el *bocadillo* |
| sandwich |

| las *patatas fritas* |
| chips |

| la *pasta* |
| pasta |

| el *arroz* |
| rice |

This page is making me really hungry

I'd be surprised if you didn't like anything on this page, which means that this vocab is important. Cover it up, scribble it down and check to see if you got it right. If not, try again.

Sweet Things and Dairy

If you've got a <u>sweet tooth</u>, this page is for you. Don't forget to learn the <u>dairy stuff</u> too, though.

Desserts — **Los postres**

Not just desserts — there's <u>other sweet stuff</u> too.

la tarta / el pastel
cake

el azúcar
sugar

el chocolate
chocolate

el helado
ice cream

la galleta
biscuit

la mermelada
jam

Learn these **dairy products**

la nata
cream

el queso
cheese

la leche
milk

el huevo
egg

el yogur
yoghurt

la mantequilla
butter

Can't get much better than a page with both cheese AND chocolate

It might be boring to talk about this food in class but imagine if you were on holiday and didn't know how to ask for an ice cream... It doesn't bear thinking about. Get this learnt.

Drinks

Okay, <u>soup</u> technically <u>isn't a drink</u> but it's <u>hot</u> and <u>liquid</u> so it's going with the <u>hot drinks</u>.

Some **cold drinks** to learn

Stick in <u>any fruit</u> from p.49 to make <u>any juice</u>.

el agua mineral
mineral water

la limonada
lemonade

el zumo/jugo de <u>naranja</u>
<u>orange</u> juice

Learn these **hot drinks**

el té
tea

el café
coffee

el café con leche
coffee with milk

la sopa
soup

el chocolate caliente
hot chocolate

A few **alcoholic drinks**

la cerveza
beer

el vino tinto
red wine

el vino blanco
white wine

This is the final page of food and drink vocab

If you thought you'd never hear the end of vocab for food and drink, you'll be pleased to know that this *is* the end. On the next page you get to put it all together in actual sentences.

Talking about Food

Here are some <u>phrases about food</u> that you can use.

I like... — Me gusta / Me gustan...

Use "<u>me gusta</u>" to say you <u>like or dislike</u> a <u>singular</u> thing.

Me gusta **la nata**. = I like <u>cream</u>.

rice: el arroz
soup: la sopa

You need to include "el", "la", "los" or "las".

No me gusta **el café**. = I don't like <u>coffee</u>.

Use "<u>me gustan</u>" for <u>plural</u> things which you <u>like or dislike</u>.

Me gustan **los plátanos**. = I like <u>bananas</u>.

carrots: las zanahorias
eggs: los huevos

To learn more about giving opinions, go to p.99.

No me gustan **las judías**. = I don't like <u>beans</u>.

More handy food vocab: *Soy* **vegetariano/a**. = I'm <u>vegetarian</u>.

Don't say you are hungry, say you **have hunger**

This is how to <u>ask</u> someone if they're <u>hungry</u> or <u>thirsty</u>:

¿Tienes **hambre?** = Are you <u>hungry</u>?   *¿Tienes* **sed?** = Are you <u>thirsty</u>?

To <u>reply</u> to these <u>questions</u>, you'd say:

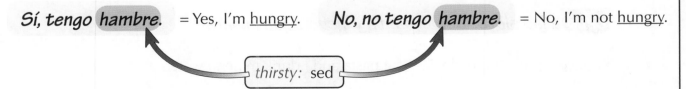

Sí, tengo **hambre**. = Yes, I'm <u>hungry</u>.   *No, no tengo* **hambre**. = No, I'm not <u>hungry</u>.

thirsty: sed

Just remember that you "have" hunger and thirst

Learn how to say that you're hungry or thirsty and also what you like and don't like to eat and drink. Even if you love all types of food, make up something that you dislike. Easy.

Talking about Food

As if you weren't <u>hungry</u> enough already, now it's time to talk about <u>mealtimes</u>.

Learn the words for mealtimes

el desayuno
breakfast

el almuerzo
lunch

la cena
evening meal

Say what you eat for each meal

Use "<u>como</u>" (I eat) and "<u>bebo</u>" (I drink) to talk about mealtimes.

Como patatas fritas. = I eat <u>chips</u>.

Bebo té. = I drink <u>tea</u>.

> *You don't need "<u>el</u>", "<u>la</u>", "<u>los</u>" or "<u>las</u>" when you say what you eat or drink. If you say something like "<u>an</u> apple" or "<u>a</u> sandwich" though, add in the "<u>un</u>" or "<u>una</u>". E.g. "como <u>una</u> manzana".*

Put the phrases together and say <u>when you eat</u> your meals:

Desayuno a las ocho. Como cereales y bebo té.

= <u>I have breakfast</u> at 8 o'clock. <u>I eat</u> cereal and <u>I drink</u> tea.

Almuerzo a la una. Como un bocadillo de queso y bebo jugo.

= <u>I have lunch</u> at 1 o'clock. <u>I eat</u> a cheese sandwich and <u>I drink</u> juice.

Ceno a las siete. Como pasta y bebo agua mineral.

= <u>I have dinner</u> at 7 o'clock. <u>I eat</u> pasta and <u>I drink</u> mineral water.

Talk about your mealtimes and what you eat and drink

I've heard that the more details you can add into a sentence, the better. So if you say what time you have breakfast, what you eat <u>and</u> what you drink, you can't go too far wrong.

In a Restaurant

If you go out for a <u>meal in Spain</u>, you're going to need the words on this page.

Learn the words for the courses

el primer plato
or **la entrada**
starter

el plato principal
main course

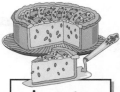

el postre
dessert

Other useful restaurant vocab

la carta
menu

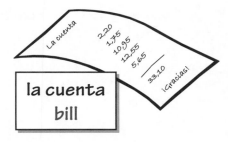

la cuenta
bill

el restaurante
restaurant

la camarera
waitress

el camarero
waiter

Learn all of this restaurant vocab so you can eat out in Spain

If you go to a Spanish restaurant, you might be really hungry and want a three course meal.
And obviously you'll need to pay the bill. That means you need to learn all this vocab.

56

In a Restaurant

If you were wondering how the restaurant vocab would come in useful, look no further.

Ask for a **table**

Una mesa para dos, por favor.   = A table for two, please.

Replace with any number, see p.1.

Order **food**

The waiter or waitress will ask you what you want like this:

This is a formal situation so the waiter uses "quiere" instead of "quieres" and you use "quisiera" instead of "quiero". For more on being polite, go to p.8-10.

¿Qué quiere tomar?   = What would you like to order?

Quisiera el filete, por favor.   = I'd like steak, please.

> *pasta:* la pasta
> *fish:* el pescado
> *chicken:* el pollo

¿Y para beber?   = Anything to drink?

Una limonada, por favor.   = Lemonade, please.

> *orange juice:* un zumo de naranja
> *mineral water:* un agua mineral

Ask for the **bill**

The waiter won't be very happy if you don't pay, so make sure you know how to ask for the bill.

La cuenta, por favor.   = The bill, please.

Use "quisiera" instead of "quiero" in a restaurant to be polite

Even if your teacher doesn't get you to do a restaurant role play, you still need to practise these phrases. Say them out loud with a friend and pretend you're going out for dinner in Spain.

Practice Questions

Track 10

Listening Question

1   Sofía is buying food for a dinner party. Listen to what she says, then write down the six things she needs to buy in English. Choose from the words in the box below.

wine	chicken	milk	tomatoes
onions	seafood	pears	chocolate
carrot	cream	potatoes	mushrooms
cheese	butter	eggs	orange juice

2   Write the Spanish words for these vegetables. Include 'el', 'la', 'los' and 'las'.

a) potato   c) cauliflower   e) peas   g) mushroom

b) carrot   d) tomato   f) beans   h) onion

3   Read this drinks list from Café Alba. Translate it into English.

> **Café Alba**
>
> té   vino tinto   limonada
> café con leche   vino blanco   agua mineral
> chocolate caliente   cerveza   zumo de naranja

4   Write these words for different foods in Spanish. Include 'el', 'la', 'los' or 'las'.

a) cereal   e) sandwich

b) chips   f) bread

c) rice   g) pasta

d) soup   h) burger

Practice Questions

5 Read the email about Esteban's likes and dislikes. In English, write one list of all the foods he likes and one list of all the food he dislikes.

> **SEND**
>
> To: julia@myemailbox.net
>
> Subject: La comida
>
> Hola Julia,
> ¿Qué tal? Voy a hablar de mi comida preferida. Me gusta el helado y el chocolate. Me gustan las fresas, las peras y los plátanos. No me gusta la lechuga y no me gusta la coliflor. No me gustan los guisantes porque son horribles y no me gusta el filete porque soy vegetariano.
> Hasta pronto, Esteban.

6 Translate these conversations into Spanish.

a)
> TOM: Ben, are you thirsty?
> BEN: No, I'm not thirsty.

b)
> ABI: Meg, are you hungry?
> MEG: Yes, I'm hungry.

7 Write these sentences about mealtimes in Spanish.

a) I have breakfast at 8 o'clock.

b) I eat cereal and drink coffee.

c) I have lunch at half past 12.

d) I eat a ham sandwich.

e) I have dinner at quarter past 7.

f) I eat chicken, rice and carrots.

8 Write the Spanish word from the box to match these clues.

a) The person who serves you. [Male *and* female version]

b) The list of dishes you can choose from.

c) The small dish eaten at the start of a meal.

d) The piece of paper which tells you how much to pay.

e) Something sweet eaten at the end of a meal.

f) The place where you go to have a meal.

g) The biggest course of the meal.

> el postre
> la carta
> el plato principal
> la cuenta
> el restaurante
> la camarera
> el primer plato
> el camarero

Clothes

Learn this page so you can talk about <u>shopping</u> (exciting) or your <u>school uniform</u> (less exciting).

Clothes — **La ropa**

una camisa
shirt

un jersey
jumper

una camiseta
T-shirt

una falda
skirt

un vestido
dress

unos calcetines
socks

unos zapatos
shoes

una chaqueta
jacket

unos vaqueros
jeans

unos pantalones
trousers

un abrigo
coat

un sombrero
hat

unos guantes
gloves

una corbata
tie

Say what you're **wearing**

Llevo + un / una / unos / unas + ITEM OF CLOTHING

Llevo un abrigo.   = I'm wearing <u>a coat</u>.

Swap this word for any of the clothes words above.

Describe what you're wearing

It may seem weird, but if you describe what you're wearing each time you wear something new, clothes vocab will become a lot easier. Keep practising until you get it all right.

Colours

Learn to say what <u>colour</u> your <u>clothes</u> are. Colours come up in <u>loads</u> of <u>other places</u>, too.

Colours — los colores

<u>Colours change</u> depending on whether the thing they <u>describe</u> is <u>masculine</u>, <u>feminine</u>, <u>singular</u> or <u>plural</u>. Learn these colours then see <u>below</u> for <u>how they change</u>.

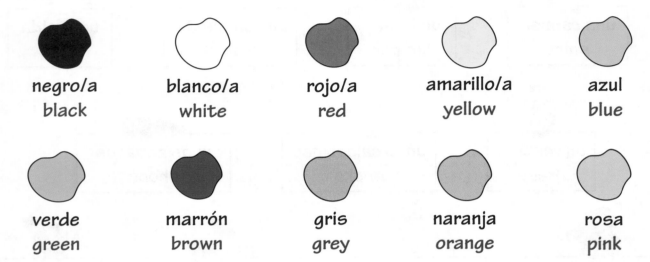

Colours ending in "o/a" change for <u>masculine</u> and <u>feminine</u> words. All the colours here change in the <u>plural form</u> — apart from "<u>naranja</u>" and "<u>rosa</u>" which <u>never</u> change.

Colours agree with the thing they describe

The <u>colour</u> goes <u>after</u> the <u>clothes word</u>. It <u>changes</u> to <u>agree</u> with what it's <u>describing</u>.

This is how to <u>describe</u> your <u>school uniform</u>:

Llevo una corbata negra*, una camisa* blanca*, un jersey* verde *y unos pantalones* grises*.*

I wear a <u>black</u> tie, a <u>white</u> shirt, a <u>green</u> jumper and <u>grey</u> trousers.

All the colours agree except for pink and orange

It's really important to learn the colours well because they crop up just about everywhere.
Practise saying what colour your school uniform is or if you don't wear one, make one up.

Asking for Things

This page is useful for <u>spending all your money</u> in those <u>lovely shops</u> in Spain.

Quisiera... — I'd like...

These are both formal ways of saying what you want. See p.8-10 for more.

Quisiera un jersey rojo. = I'd like <u>a red jumper</u>.

Add "por favor" at the end to make these more polite.

¿Tiene un jersey rojo? = Do you have <u>a red jumper</u>?

Some other useful shopping phrases

¿Algo más? = Anything else?

✓ *Sí, por favor.* = Yes, please.

✗ *No, gracias.* = No, thank you.

When you want to buy something

To say "<u>I'll buy it</u>" in Spanish, you need to know if the item of clothing is <u>masculine</u> or <u>feminine</u>.

1) If the thing you do (or don't) want to buy is <u>masculine</u>, (e.g. "un sombrero"), you say:

✓ *Lo compro.* = I'll buy <u>it</u>.

✗ *No lo compro.* = I won't buy <u>it</u>.

*"<u>Lo</u>" is a <u>direct object pronoun</u> (see p.108). It <u>replaces</u> the <u>noun</u>, e.g. "un sombrero" (a hat).
For a <u>masculine plural</u> noun, like "unos guantes" (gloves), you'd say "<u>los</u> compro".*

2) If the thing you're replacing is <u>feminine</u> (e.g. "una falda"), you'd say:

✓ *La compro.* = I'll buy <u>it</u>.

✗ *No la compro.* = I won't buy <u>it</u>.

You can change "<u>la</u>" for "<u>las</u>" if the noun you're replacing is <u>feminine plural</u>.

Learn these shopping phrases — they come in very handy

This page will be really useful if you find yourself drawn to the high street in a Spanish city.
Remember how to say "I won't buy it" too — you don't <u>need</u> to buy it all...

Prices

If you decide that you do want to buy those jeans, you'd better <u>ask how much they cost</u>.

Ask **how much** something **costs**

Use this to find out the <u>price</u> of something.

¿Cuánto cuesta? = How much is it?

> *Watch out if the thing you want to buy is <u>plural</u> though — you have to <u>change</u> "cuesta" to "cuestan".*

¿Cuánto cuestan los vaqueros? = How much are the jeans?

This is how the <u>shopkeeper</u> would <u>reply</u>:

Cuesta veintiocho euros. = It's <u>twenty-eight</u> euros.

If the thing you want to buy is <u>plural</u> (e.g. "los vaqueros") "<u>cuesta</u>" changes to "<u>cuestan</u>", e.g. "<u>cuestan</u> veintiocho euros".

Spanish money is in **Euros**

Spanish money's easy. There are <u>100 cents</u> in a <u>euro</u>, like there are <u>100 pence</u> in a <u>pound</u>.

This what the euro symbol looks like...

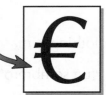

...and these are euro notes and coins.

This is what you'd <u>see</u> on a Spanish <u>price tag</u> — they use a <u>comma</u>, not a decimal point:

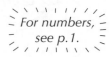

> *For numbers, see p.1.*

This is how you <u>say</u> the <u>price</u>:

Cinco euros con cincuenta (céntimos).

= <u>Five</u> euros <u>fifty</u> (cents).

"Euros" is pronounced "ey-oo-ross" in Spanish

The key to being able to say how much something costs (or understanding a price when someone tells you) is knowing your numbers. So all you've got to do is keep practising them.

Practice Questions

Track 11   <u>Listening Question</u>

1   Juan is shopping for clothes. Listen to his conversation with the
shop assistant and answer the questions below in English.

  a)   What colour shoes does Juan ask for?

  b)   What is the second item of clothing that he asks for?

  c)   What colour is the second item of clothing that he buys?

  d)   How much does he pay for his clothes in total?

2   Write the Spanish for these clothes. Include 'el', 'la', 'los' and 'las'.

  a) trousers   c) shirt   e) skirt   g) dress   i) T-shirt

  b) jumper   d) socks   f) hat   h) jacket   j) shoes

3   Copy and complete the descriptions of these outfits by translating the bits in
brackets into Spanish. Make sure all the adjectives agree correctly.

  a)

  > Llevo una falda *[green]*, un *[jumper]* naranja, un sombrero *[blue]*,
  > unos zapatos *[red]* y unos calcetines *[yellow]*.

  b)

  > Llevo unos *[trousers]* rojos, una camisa *[pink]*, una corbata *[white]*,
  > una *[jacket]* marrón, unos *[socks]* negros y unos zapatos *[grey]*.

4   Write the correct number next to each letter to match the Spanish
phrases on the left to their English meanings on the right.

  a) ¿Algo más?   **1**   I would like a skirt.

  b) ¿Tiene calcetines?   **2**   I'll buy it.

  c) Cuesta veinte euros.   **3**   How much is it?

  d) Lo compro.   **4**   Do you have any socks?

  e) ¿Cuánto cuesta?   **5**   Anything else?

  f) Quisiera una falda.   **6**   It costs twenty euros.

Summary Questions

Another set of questions to answer — lucky you. There's a lot of vocab to learn in this section so take your time, go through the questions slowly and make sure you look up any answers you get wrong.

1) Write down two ways of asking someone how to get to the bank in Spanish.

2) What do these mean in English?
   a) gire a la izquierda   b) tome la primera calle a la derecha

3) Translate this conversation into Spanish.
   Helen: "Where is the market?"
   Simon: "Turn right, go straight on, take the second street on the left."
   Helen: "Is it far from here?"
   Simon: "It's two kilometres from here."

4) Write down the names of these places in Spanish: (Don't forget the 'el and 'la' bits.)
   a) butcher's   b) cake shop   c) newsagent's   d) library   e) sweet shop   f) grocer's

5) What is the English for these shops?
   a) la panadería   b) el supermercado   c) el mercado   d) el banco   e) la farmacia

6) What are these places called in English?
   a) la estación   b) la iglesia   c) el museo   d) el hospital   e) la oficina de turismo

7) Write these places down in Spanish:
   a) post office   b) cinema   c) castle   d) town hall   e) leisure centre   f) theatre

8) What are these foods in Spanish?
   a)   b)   c)   d)   e)   f)   g)

9) Choose four of your favourite (or least favourite) vegetables and write them down in Spanish.

10) How would you say these in Spanish?
    a) pork   b) lamb   c) beef   d) chicken   e) ham   f) sausage   g) fish

11) How do you say this list of sweet things: *cake, chocolate, biscuit, sugar, ice-cream, jam*

12) Write these drinks down in Spanish: *tea, coffee, hot chocolate, lemonade, orange juice, beer*

13) In Spanish, write four sentences about what foods you like and four about foods you don't like.

14) Juan asks you "¿Tienes hambre?". How would you answer? Ask him if he's thirsty.

15) Write down what and when you usually eat for breakfast, lunch and dinner. In Spanish.

16) Write these words in Spanish:
    a) bill   b) waitress   c) waiter   d) restaurant   e) menu   f) main course

17) Write this conversation out in Spanish:
    Ana: "A table for five, please." Waiter: "What would you like?" Ana: "I'd like the pasta."

18) Say what you're wearing by completing this sentence: "Llevo..." Say what colour everything is.

19) Write this final conversation out in Spanish: *Ed: "Do you have a green hat?"*
    — Shop assistant: "Yes, anything else?" — *Ed: "No, I'll take it."*

Sport

At KS3, it's common to get asked about <u>sports and hobbies</u> — you'll need this vocab.

Sports — **Los deportes**

Here are a few <u>popular</u> sports to get you started.

| **el hockey** |
| hockey |

| **el tenis de mesa / el ping-pong** |
| table tennis |

| **el baloncesto** |
| basketball |

| **el fútbol** |
| football |

| **el rugby** |
| rugby |

| **el ajedrez** |
| chess |

| **el tenis** |
| tennis |

Say what you play — **Juego...**

Juego + al + SPORT

*"<u>al</u>" = "<u>a</u> + <u>el</u>" (see p.105)
If you had a "<u>la</u>" sport, you
would say "juego <u>a la</u>..."*

Juego al fútbol.

= I play <u>football</u>.

This should be a fun page for you sporty types

As well as learning all the sports vocab, make sure you feel comfortable using "juego al..." phrases. Even if you don't play sports, pretend you do so you can practise this stuff too.

Musical Instruments

Right, that's <u>sport</u> out of the way. Time for some <u>culture</u>...

Instruments — Los instrumentos

This stuff is particularly useful for any <u>budding musicians</u> out there — though of course, <u>everyone</u> needs to learn this for KS3 Spanish.

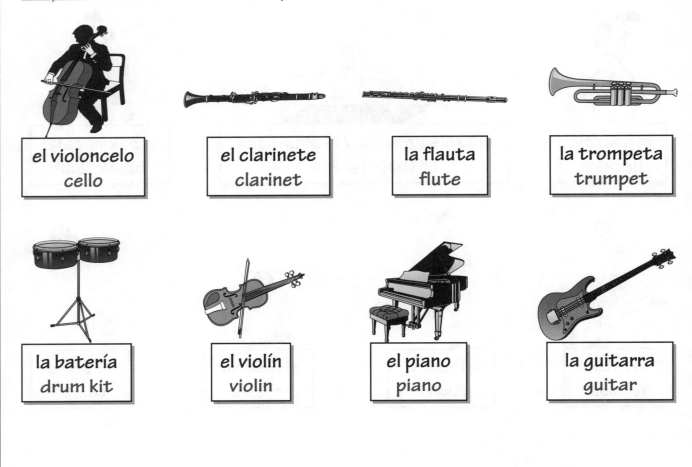

| **el violoncelo** cello | **el clarinete** clarinet | **la flauta** flute | **la trompeta** trumpet |

| **la batería** drum kit | **el violín** violin | **el piano** piano | **la guitarra** guitar |

Say what you play — Toco...

Toco + el / la + INSTRUMENT

Important: Use "<u>jugar</u>" for sports, and "<u>tocar</u>" for musical instruments.

Toco la trompeta.

= I play <u>the trumpet</u>.

"Toco" is for instruments and "juego" is for sports

This is a really important difference that you have to get right — or you won't make any sense at all in Spanish. Practise lots of phrases, even if you don't play any sports or instruments.

Pastimes and Hobbies

With these hobbies, instead of saying "I play..." you say, "I do..." or "I go..."

I do... — Hago...

"Hago" is the Spanish verb for "I do". Use "hago" for these hobbies:

Hago ciclismo.
I *go* cycling.

Hago esquí.
I *go* skiing.

Hago senderismo.
I *go* hiking.

Hago aerobic.
I *do* aerobics.

Hago footing.
I *go* jogging.

I go... — Voy...

"Voy" is the Spanish verb for "I go". Use "voy" for these hobbies:

See p.124 for more on the verb "voy".

Voy a nadar. = I go swimming.

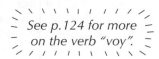

Voy de compras. = I go shopping.

"Voy de compras" is shopping for fun — not like "Hago la compra" on p.25 which is grocery shopping.

If you don't have any hobbies, you'll have to pretend you do

Practise the vocab you're most likely to use, but make sure you know the other ones too. They're bound to crop up in listening or reading exercises and you need to be prepared.

Pastimes and Hobbies

If you'd rather <u>curl up on the sofa</u> than play sports, then this page is for you.

I watch television — **Veo la televisión**

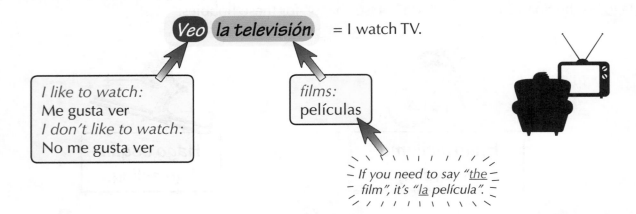

Veo **la televisión.** = I watch TV.

I like to watch:
Me gusta ver
I don't like to watch:
No me gusta ver

films: películas

~ If you need to say "<u>the</u> ~
~ film", it's "<u>la</u> película". ~

I listen to music — **Escucho música**

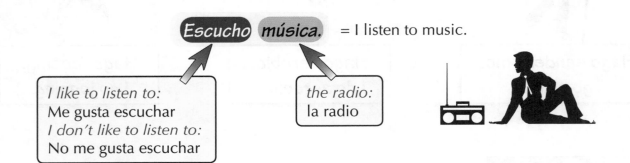

Escucho **música.** = I listen to music.

I like to listen to:
Me gusta escuchar
I don't like to listen to:
No me gusta escuchar

the radio:
la radio

I read books — **Leo libros**

If you need to say "<u>the</u> books" etc, the articles are: "<u>los</u> libros", "<u>las</u> revistas", "<u>los</u> periódicos", "<u>las</u> novelas".

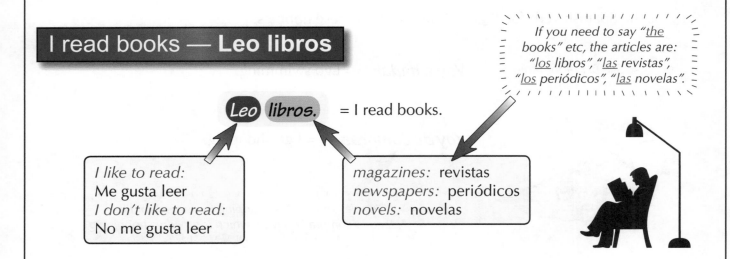

Leo **libros.** = I read books.

I like to read:
Me gusta leer
I don't like to read:
No me gusta leer

magazines: revistas
newspapers: periódicos
novels: novelas

Learn all these indoors-y activities

There's actually quite a bit of vocab packed away in this page, so make sure you learn it all. Practise giving your opinion too — it's a fail safe way to get extra credit in Spanish work.

Likes and Dislikes

Opinions will get you lots of marks in Spanish, so learn this stuff and use it whenever you can.

Do you like tennis? — ¿Te gusta el tenis?

Here's how to say what you think of the different sports and hobbies on p.65 and p.67.
You can replace the highlighted words with just about anything you like.

For more on opinions, see p.99-100.

¿Te gusta **el tenis?**

= Do you like tennis?

Me gusta **el tenis** ...

= I like tennis...

No me gusta **el tenis** ...

= I don't like tennis...

...porque es **interesante.**

= ...because it's interesting.

easy: fácil
fun: divertido/a

...porque es **aburrido.**

= ...because it's boring.

difficult: difícil
tiring: cansado/a

I like this film — Me gusta esta película

You can also give your opinion on something specific you've seen or read:

Me gusta **esta película.**

= I like this film.

this music: esta música
this book: este libro
this newspaper: este periódico

No me gusta **esta película.**

= I don't like this film.

See p.115 for more on "esta" and "este".

Talk about your likes and dislikes whenever you can

Knowing loads of vocab is great, but it's much more useful to be able to say that you like or don't like something. If you can give a reason to back up your opinion, that's even better.

Practice Questions

      <u>Listening Question</u>

1   Alicia, Felipe and Begoña are talking about their hobbies.
Listen to what each person says, then answer the questions below.

     a)   What sport does Alicia do?

     b)   What does Alicia read?

     c)   What sport does Felipe play with his friends?

     d)   What does Felipe like to watch?

     e)   What two instruments does Begoña play?

     f)   What does Begoña not like to read?

2   Complete each of these sentences using either 'toco' or 'juego'.

     a)   .... al baloncesto con mis amigos.

     b)   .... la flauta en la orquesta de mi instituto.

     c)   .... la guitarra todos los días.

     d)   .... al ajedrez con mi padre.

     e)   .... al tenis porque es divertido.

3   Write these sentences in Spanish.

     a)   I play the cello.   c)   I play rugby.

     b)   I play basketball.   d)   I play the drums.

4   Copy and complete these sentences by writing the words in brackets in Spanish.

     a)   Me gusta *[to go cycling]* porque es *[easy]*.

     b)   No me gusta *[to go hiking]* porque es *[boring]*.   HINT: the infinitive of the verb "hago" is "hacer".

     c)   Me encanta *[to do aerobics]* porque es *[fun]*.

     d)   Odio *[to go jogging]* porque es *[difficult]*.

5   Write in Spanish how you would say:

     a)   I like this film.   c)   I like this book.

     b)   I don't like this film.   d)   I don't like this book.

Places to Go

The information on the next few pages has everything you need to <u>organise a day out</u> in Spain — almost. You'll also need a couple of willing Spanish friends to invite along.

Pick a **place to go**

Pick your <u>dream destination</u> — within reason.
Here are some common places you might go with friends.

el restaurante
the restaurant

el cine
the cinema

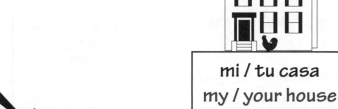

mi / tu casa
my / your house

el centro
the town centre

el teatro
the theatre

la piscina
the swimming pool

el polideportivo
the leisure centre

el parque
the park

Cover up the labels and test yourself

This vocab can come in really handy. For example, if someone's giving you directions (see p.45) or describing where something is, they might use these places as reference points.

Going Out and Making Arrangements

Suggest a <u>trip out</u> or learn what to say if someone invites you to go out.

Let's go to... — **Vamos...**

Use this to say, "<u>Let's go to...</u>"

Use "<u>al</u>" for "<u>el</u>" words, and "<u>a la</u>" for "<u>la</u>" words. See p.105 for more.

Vamos + al / a la + PLACE

Vamos a la piscina.

= Let's go <u>to the</u> <u>swimming pool</u>.

There's an <u>exception</u> you need to learn — and that's for going to <u>someone's house</u>.

*Vamos a **mi** casa.*   = Let's go to <u>my</u> house.

*Vamos a **tu** casa.*   = Let's go to <u>your</u> house.

You don't need "<u>al</u>" or "<u>a la</u>" with "<u>mi</u>" or "<u>tu</u>". See p.114 for more on "my", "your" etc.

Learn how to **accept** or **reject** an invitation

Learn this, and then if someone <u>asks you</u> to go somewhere, you can <u>answer them</u>.
As always, if you <u>give a reason</u> for saying "yes" or "no", you'll sound really good.

'YES' PHRASES

Yes, of course:
Sí, por supuesto
Good idea:
Buena idea
Great!:
¡Estupendo!

'NO' PHRASES

No, thank you:
No gracias
I don't like the swimming pool:
No me gusta la piscina
I don't have any money:
No tengo dinero

Let's go to your house to do our homework

The "yes" and "no" phrases on this page are useful in lots of situations and you're probably going to hear them quite a lot at KS3. So test yourself to make sure you've learnt them all.

Going Out and Making Arrangements

Learn this page or be left <u>stranded for hours</u> wondering why no one has shown up.

Where shall we meet? — ¿Dónde nos encontramos?

You can suggest just about <u>anywhere you like</u>:

Nos encontramos en el restaurante. = Let's meet <u>at the restaurant</u>.

> *at the swimming pool:* en la piscina
> *in the town centre:* en el centro

You need to use "en" before the place you want to meet.

Nos encontramos delante del cine. = Let's meet <u>in front of the cinema</u>.

Phrases like "in front of" are called prepositions. See p.141 for more.

> *in front of the theatre:* delante del teatro

When shall we meet? — ¿Cuándo nos encontramos?

You can suggest a <u>specific time</u> to meet:

Nos encontramos a las ocho. = Let's meet <u>at eight o'clock</u>.

Use any clock time here — see p.2.

Or use a <u>more general</u> time phrase:

Nos encontramos esta noche. = Let's meet <u>tonight</u>.

> *this afternoon:* esta tarde
> *tomorrow:* mañana
> *on Monday:* el lunes

See p.3 for days of the week.

Experiment with as many combinations as you can

Learning just one or two examples isn't really going to do your Spanish many favours — learn a range of vocab so you can feel confident using lots of different places and time phrases.

Going Out and Making Arrangements

Not much is <u>free</u> these days, so you'll probably need to <u>buy a ticket</u>.

Buying tickets

¿Cuánto cuesta una entrada? = How much does a ticket cost?

Una entrada cuesta cuatro euros. = A ticket costs four euros.

Quisiera una entrada, por favor. = I'd like <u>one ticket</u>, please.

> *two tickets:* dos entradas
> *three tickets:* tres entradas

Finally, put it **all together...**

Using the vocab from the last few pages, this is what a conversation <u>might look like</u>:

Vamos al polideportivo.

= Let's go to the sports centre.

¡Genial! Me encantan los deportes.

= Great! I love sports.

See p.99 for "me encanta".

¿Dónde nos encontramos?

= Where shall we meet?

Nos encontramos en tu casa.

= Let's meet at your house.

¿Cuándo nos encontramos?

= What time shall we meet?

Nos encontramos a las cuatro y media.

= Let's meet at half past four.

The most sociable page in the book

"Making plans" is a common topic for teachers to use in speaking practice. Get ahead and nail this vocab by doing a role play with your friend, class-mate or even your own reflection...

Transport

It's time to get from <u>A to B</u>. Pick your favourite <u>form of transport</u> here.

Learn the names of these **vehicles**

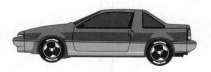

| el coche |
| car |

| la bicicleta |
| bike |

| el autobús |
| bus |

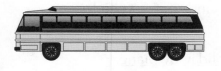

| el autocar |
| coach |

| el tren |
| train |

| el metro |
| the underground |

| el avión |
| plane |

| el barco |
| boat |

| la motocicleta |
| motorbike |

There are only nine of these words to learn

Transport vocab is really useful stuff, trust me. And if you don't think this is useful now, wait until you decide to go back-packing around South America in six years' time...

Transport

This page will show you how to put the words for <u>types of transport</u> into <u>useful phrases</u>.

I go by... — **Voy en...**

Use this <u>simple formula</u> to say how you <u>get to places</u>.

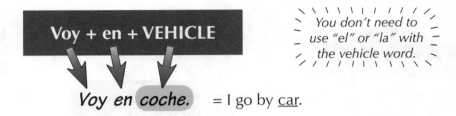

Voy + en + VEHICLE

You don't need to use "el" or "la" with the vehicle word.

Voy en coche. = I go by <u>car</u>.

You can use this formula with <u>almost every</u> method of transport except walking (see below).

Voy en tren. = I go by <u>train</u>.   **Voy en autobús.** = I go by <u>bus</u>.

You can also use this formula to say <u>how you get to school</u> or <u>how you go on holiday</u>. The bit about <u>where you're going</u> gets sandwiched between "<u>Voy</u>" and "<u>en</u>" + vehicle.

Voy de vacaciones en avión. = I go <u>on holiday</u> by <u>plane</u>.

You can put any method of transport here.

Voy al instituto en bicicleta. = I go <u>to school</u> by <u>bike</u>.

There's a special phrase for walking

Of course, there's one <u>exception</u>. It's an important one, so learn it well.

Voy a pie. = I go <u>on foot</u>.

Practise this with all the different types of transport

If you really want to push yourself, practise saying <u>where</u> you go as well. Remember, the destination goes in the middle of the formula. For example, "Voy al supermercado en coche".

Transport

Learn this and next time you're in Spain you can get yourself a ticket to <u>somewhere fabulous</u>.

Learn how to **ask about a journey**

Here are some <u>useful questions</u> you might want to ask if you're catching a bus or train.
There are some <u>example answers</u> to help you too.

(1) ¿Hay **un tren** para Madrid? = Is there <u>a train</u> to Madrid?

Instead of "<u>un tren</u>", you might say "<u>un autocar</u>" or "<u>un autobús</u>".

(2) ¿Cuándo sale el tren para Madrid? | ¿Cuándo llega el tren a Madrid?

= When does the train to Madrid leave? | = When does the train arrive in Madrid?

El tren para Madrid sale / llega a las diez.

= The train to Madrid leaves / arrives at ten o'clock.

(3) ¿De qué andén sale el tren? = Which platform does the train leave from?

El tren sale del andén número dos. = The train leaves from platform two.

Learn these **types of ticket**

Learn this vocab, then use the example to make a <u>complete sentence</u> asking for a ticket.

un billete de ida / un billete sencillo a single ticket	un billete de ida y vuelta a return ticket	de primera clase first class	de segunda clase second class

Quisiera un billete de ida, de segunda clase para Madrid, por favor.

= I would like <u>a single ticket</u>, <u>second class</u> to Madrid please.

This vocab is your key to the open road

Even if you're not much of a traveller, you'll need this vocab for reading and listening exercises. So basically, you still have to learn all the questions and ticket types on this page. Sorry.

Practice Questions

Listening Questions

1   Listen to Andrés and Luisa making arrangements to go out
     and then answer the questions below in English.

     a)   Where does Luisa not want to go?

     b)   Where do Andrés and Luisa agree to go?

     c)   Where do they arrange to meet?

     d)   At what time do they arrange to meet?

     e)   How much does a ticket cost?

2   Listen to this conversation between a station employee and a passenger
     at a railway station. Answer the questions below in English.

     a)   What time does the train to Pamplona leave?

     b)   Which platform does it leave from?

     c)   What time will the train arrive in Pamplona?

     d)   What kind of ticket does the passenger want? Give two details.

     e)   How much does the ticket cost?

3   Where would you go if you wanted to do the following things?
     Write the correct Spanish word from the box.

     a)   to have a good meal

     b)   to go swimming

     c)   to watch a play

     d)   to walk the dog

     e)   to see a film

     f)   to play indoor sports

     g)   to go to bed

mi casa
el teatro
el polideportivo
el parque
el restaurante
la piscina
el cine

Practice Questions

4   Read the following arrangements for going out then copy and complete the grid below in English. The first one has been done for you.

Nos encontramos en el centro a las once menos cuarto.

Rubén

Nos encontramos delante de la piscina a las diez y cuarto.

Yolanda

Nos encontramos en el teatro a las ocho y media.

Carmen

Nos encontramos en mi casa a las tres.

Patricio

Nos encontramos delante del cine a las nueve.

Iker

Person	Meeting Place	Time
Rubén	*in the town centre*	*10.45*
Carmen		
Iker		
Yolanda		
Patricio		

5   Copy and complete the transport page in Manolo's vocabulary book.

Spanish	English
el autobús	
	coach
el avión	
	boat

Spanish	English
	car
el metro	
	motorbike
la bicicleta	

6   Using the key, write out how you'd ask for each of the following train tickets.

Key: → single   ⇄ return

For example: → Valencia 2nd

Quisiera un billete de ida, de segunda clase, para Valencia.

a) → Segovia, 1st   b) ⇄ Ávila, 1st   c) ⇄ Cuenca, 2nd

Summary Questions

This section covers a fair few different things, from chess to train tickets, from clarinets to swimming pools. Now it's time to test if all that info has sunk in. And if it hasn't, go back over this section and do the questions again until you get them 100% right.

1) Write the names of these sports in Spanish:
   a) hockey   b) table tennis   c) football   d) tennis

2) Write these sentences out in Spanish:
   a) I play the clarinet.   b) I play chess.   c) I play the trumpet.

3) How do you say these things in Spanish?
   a) I go jogging.   b) I go hiking.   c) I go shopping.   d) I go cycling.

4) Answer this question in Spanish and give a reason for your answer:
   "¿Te gusta el hockey?"

5) What does "Me gusta ver películas" mean in English?

6) Write down what these mean in English:
   a) las revistas   b) los libros   c) las novelas   d) los periódicos

7) How would you say these phrases in Spanish?
   a) I like this magazine.   b) I like this music.

8) Write the names of these places in Spanish:
   a) the park   b) the swimming pool   c) the leisure centre   d) my house

9) You're with your Spanish friend Lucas. Say "Let's go to the theatre."

10) Lucas says, "Sí, por supuesto." What does that mean in English?

11) In Spanish, tell Lucas you'll meet in front of the theatre at half past eight.

12) You and Lucas are at the theatre. How do you ask how much a ticket costs?

13) Write what these words are in Spanish:
    a) bike   b) boat   c) the underground   d) plane   e) coach

14) In Spanish, how do you say:
    a) I go on foot   b) I go by car   c) I go by bus   d) I go by bike

15) You're at the bus station in Valencia.
    a) How do you ask if there's a bus to Benidorm?
    b) How do you ask what time the bus to Benidorm leaves?
    c) How do you ask what time the bus arrives in Benidorm?

16) You decide you want a return train ticket to Benidorm, first class.
    How do you ask for this in Spanish?

At the Post Office

Getting postcards is <u>great</u> — you can learn how to <u>send</u> them with the useful vocab on this page.

At the post office — En la oficina de Correos

The vocab below is for things you might want from the <u>post office</u>.

un sello
a stamp

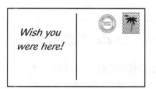

una postal
a postcard

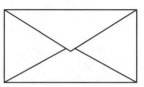

un sobre
an envelope

un buzón
a postbox

una carta
a letter

la dirección
the address

Learn these useful sentences

The vocab above isn't enough on its own — learn these <u>sentences</u> as well.

Quisiera mandar una carta a Inglaterra. *¿Cuánto cuesta?*

= I would like to send a letter to <u>England</u>. How much is that?

Quisiera un sello para Inglaterra *por favor.*

= I would like a stamp for <u>England</u>, please.

Change "Inglaterra" to any country you need. *See p.94 for country names.*

Now you've got no excuse not to send your Gran a postcard

If you're not off on holiday to Spain any time soon, you'll still need this vocab for KS3 Spanish — so cover up those labels and test yourself on that vocab. C'mon, you can do it...

Telephones

Being able to use the phone is practically a survival skill, so it's worth learning this stuff well.

Telephone numbers — Los números de teléfono

The most useful phone number to learn is your own.

| el número de teléfono |
| telephone number |

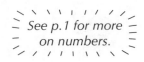
See p.1 for more on numbers.

In Spanish, you introduce telephone numbers with "el" and you say the number in groups of two, i.e. twenty-eight rather than two, eight.

Mi número de teléfono es el cuarenta y nueve, sesenta, veintitrés.

= My telephone number is 496023.

How to **talk on the phone** in Spanish

These are some basic phrases that you might need to have a phone conversation in Spanish.

1) This is how you answer the phone:

   ¡Dígame!   = Hello?

2) This is how to say who you are:

   Hola, soy Tamara.   = Hello, it's Tamara.

3) And this is how to ask to speak to someone:

   ¿Puedo hablar con Marco?   = Can I speak to Marco?

The telephone — great for a chat and vital in emergencies

From booking meals in restaurants to making plans with friends, using the phone in Spanish is a brilliant skill for holidays. It's also key for success in KS3 Spanish — so get learning.

Informal Letters

Informal letters are to people you <u>already know</u> well, or people the <u>same age as you</u>.
For example, <u>postcards</u>, friendly <u>e-mails</u>, or messages on <u>social network pages</u>.

Start a letter with "**Querido/a**" — "Dear..."

This is a really <u>basic</u> layout for a <u>letter</u>.

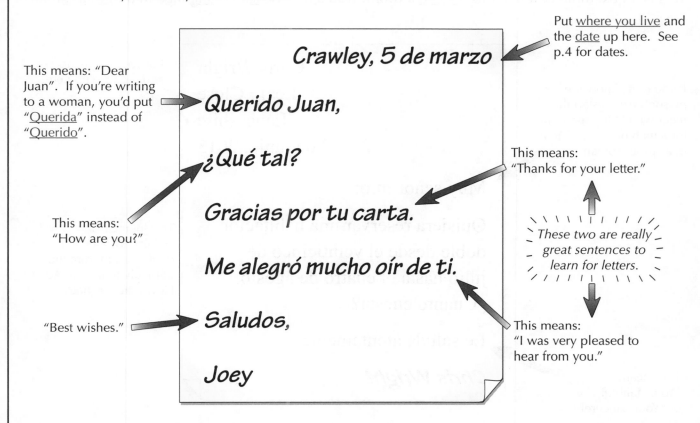

Put <u>where you live</u> and the <u>date</u> up here. See p.4 for dates.

Crawley, 5 de marzo

This means: "Dear Juan". If you're writing to a woman, you'd put "<u>Querida</u>" instead of "<u>Querido</u>".

Querido Juan,

¿Qué tal?

This means: "How are you?"

Gracias por tu carta.

This means: "Thanks for your letter."

These two are really great sentences to learn for letters.

Me alegró mucho oír de ti.

"Best wishes."

Saludos,

This means: "I was very pleased to hear from you."

Joey

Other phrases to use in letters

Put these at the <u>end</u> of <u>informal</u> letters, postcards and e-mails.
You can use them <u>instead of "saludos"</u>.

This one is for people you know really well.

Escríbeme pronto.

= Write soon.

Hasta pronto.

= Bye for now.

Un abrazo.

= A hug.

Even if you don't write letters, this stuff is still relevant

Lots of the handy phrases on this page are suitable for chatting with young people in Spanish.
They're as good for online messages as they are for real letters, so don't be afraid to use them.

Formal Letters

In formal situations, you need to use the right kind of language.

Learn these set phrases for formal letters

Formal letters include things like booking hotel rooms (see p.90) or writing to companies. This is an example of a letter to reserve a room. You'd use the same language in a formal e-mail.

Put your name, address and the date up here.

Chris Wright
Leafy Close
Lancashire
2 de junio, 2013

If you don't know the person's name, start the letter with "Muy señor mío" for a man or "Muy señora mía" for a woman.

Muy señor mío:

Quisiera reservar una habitación doble desde el veinticinco de julio hasta el cuatro de agosto. ¿Cuánto cuesta?

This lot means: "I'd like to reserve a double room from the 25th July to the 4th August. How much is that?"

Le saluda atentamente,

Chris Wright

This means: "Yours faithfully" or "Yours sincerely".

Another way of starting a formal letter

If you do know the name of the person you're writing to, use "Estimado" or "Estimada". "Estimado" is for a man and "Estimada" is for a woman.

Estimado señor García   = Dear Mr García

Estimada señora Panza   = Dear Mrs Panza

You'll thank yourself later if you learn these set phrases now

That way, when you need to write a letter, you'll only need to think about the vocab for the other stuff — like booking a campsite or writing to an exchange partner's parents. Marvellous.

Practice Questions

1 These Spanish words for things in the post office have been scrambled.
Write them out correctly with the matching word in English from the box.
For example: nu lesol *un sello = a stamp*

a) aun atcra   d) la icróndice

b) uan slopat   e) un ebros

c) nu nuzób

a letter	a postcard
an envelope	a postbox
the address	~~a stamp~~

2 Here are some phrases from informal letters, but some of the words are missing.
Copy and complete each sentence using the words in the box.

a) Thanks for your letter.   .... por tu ....

b) Dear John, ... John,

c) A hug   Un ....

d) How are you?   ¿Qué ....?

e) Write soon.   .... pronto.

escríbeme	tal
carta	gracias
abrazo	querido

3 Write an informal letter to your friend Ana, including the details below.

- The date and place of writing
- Greet Ana
- Ask her how she is
- Thank her for her letter
- Tell her you were very pleased to hear from her
- Tell her to write soon
- Send her best wishes
- Sign your name

HINT: Look back to p.83 for a reminder of how to lay out a letter.

4 In the box are some useful phrases for writing formal letters.
Write the number of the phrase you would use:

a) to write to a woman whose name you know

b) to write the place and date of writing

c) to write to a man whose name you don't know

d) to sign off your letter 'yours faithfully'

1) Estimada señora...
2) Muy señora mía
3) Muy señor mío
4) Crewe, 20 de mayo
5) Le saluda atentamente
6) Hasta pronto

Summary Questions

Just because this was a short section, it doesn't mean it was less important, or that there's not a bundle of questions for you at the end. Cover the info on the pages and have a go at these. And yes — make sure you repeat them until you get all the answers right.

1) How would you ask for an envelope in Spanish?

2) In Spanish, how would you ask for two stamps to England?

3) How would you say "I'd like to send a letter to London?" in Spanish.

4) What's the Spanish word for "address"?

5) How would you give your phone number in Spanish?
   Make sure you use the right format.

6) How would you give your mobile phone number in Spanish?
   Again, make sure you use the right format.

7) You're writing a letter to a friend called Ruben, who you met on holiday.
   How would you greet Ruben at the start of the letter?

8) How would you tell Ruben to write soon in Spanish?

9) List three phrases in Spanish that you could use at the end of your informal letter.

10) How would you begin a formal letter in Spanish to a woman whose name you <u>don't</u> know?

11) How would you begin a formal letter in Spanish to a woman whose name is Señora Sopeña?

12) You want to write a letter to Mr Rodríguez, a teacher at a Spanish school.
    How would you start your letter?

13) How would you write "yours sincerely" in Spanish?

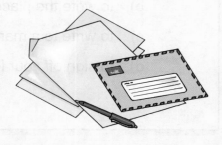

Weather and Seasons

Make sure you learn whether the <u>different types of weather</u> go with "<u>hace</u>", "<u>está</u>" or "<u>hay</u>".

What's the weather like? — ¿Qué tiempo hace?

Hace +

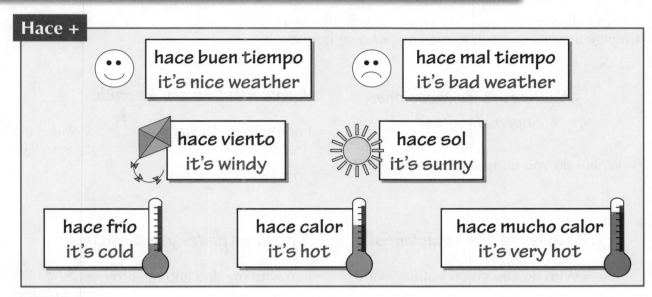

hace buen tiempo it's nice weather	**hace mal tiempo** it's bad weather
hace viento it's windy	**hace sol** it's sunny

hace frío it's cold

hace calor it's hot

hace mucho calor it's very hot

Está +

está nevando it's snowing

está nublado it's cloudy

está lloviendo it's raining

Hay +

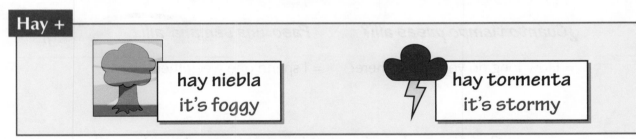

hay niebla it's foggy

hay tormenta it's stormy

The seasons — Las estaciones

la primavera spring

el verano summer

el otoño autumn

el invierno winter

Siempre hace buen tiempo — not where I live

British people love talking about the weather so now you have the perfect opportunity to talk about it even more, and in Spanish. Practise saying what the weather's like each day.

Holidays

Teachers love to ask about <u>holidays</u> so this page is really useful for helping you <u>answer</u> them.

Talk about where you **normally** go on **holiday**

The <u>blue bits</u> are the <u>questions</u> and the <u>yellow bits</u> are the <u>answers</u>.
Change the bits in <u>green</u> to match your <u>own holiday</u>.

¿Adónde vas de vacaciones normalmente?

= Where do you normally go on holiday?

Normalmente voy a España.

= I normally go to <u>Spain</u>.

For other countries, see p.94.

¿Con quién vas de vacaciones?

= Who do you go on holiday with?

Voy con mi padre y mi hermano.

= I go with <u>my dad and my brother</u>.

For other people, see p.15.

¿Dónde te quedas?

= Where do you stay?

Me quedo en un hotel.

= I stay in <u>a hotel</u>.

For other places to stay, see p.89.

¿Cuánto tiempo pasas allí?

= How long do you spend there?

Paso una semana allí.

= I spend <u>one week</u> there.

For other times, see p.3.

¿Qué tiempo hace?

= What is the weather like?

Hace sol y mucho calor.

= <u>It's sunny and very hot</u>.

For more weather, see p.87.

¿Qué haces allí?

= What do you do there?

Voy a la playa.

= <u>I go to the beach</u>.

For other activities, see p.67.

Remember to answer these questions in full sentences

No doubt you'll do holiday role plays in class so get practising these sentences. Make sure you change the bits in the green boxes so that your answers aren't the same as everyone else's.

Hotels and Camping

If you have the luxury of <u>staying in a hotel</u> when you're on <u>holiday</u>, this page is very <u>important</u>.

Some **places to stay**

el hotel
hotel

el albergue juvenil
youth hostel

el camping
campsite

At the hotel — **En el hotel**

Here's some <u>vocab</u> about types of <u>hotel rooms</u>:

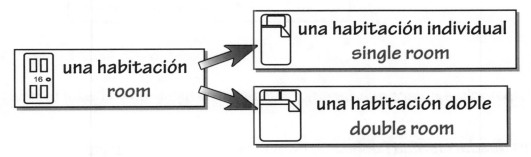

una habitación
room

una habitación individual
single room

una habitación doble
double room

Una habitación con baño. = A <u>room</u> with <u>a bath</u>.

single room: habitación individual
double room: habitación doble

balcony: balcón
shower: ducha

Here's some more <u>really useful</u> hotel vocab:

los servicios
toilets

la llave
key

el teléfono
telephone

el comedor
dining room

Learn this vocab well so you can book a room in a hotel

Okay, this is just a page of hotel vocab but it's really important that you learn it well so that when it comes to booking a single room with a balcony (on p.90) you'll be ready to go.

Hotels and Camping

Here are all the <u>questions</u> and <u>answers</u> you'll need to <u>book a holiday</u>. Take your time.

Booking a **hotel room** — tell them **what** and **when**

The <u>yellow bits</u> are what <u>you'd say</u> and the <u>blue bits</u> are what the <u>hotel receptionist</u> would say.
<u>Change</u> the bits in <u>green</u> to match what you want.

The questions here are in the <u>polite form</u>. For more, go to p.8-10.

(1)   *¿Tiene una habitación libre?*   = Do you have any free rooms?

(2)   *¿Qué tipo de habitación quiere?*   = What type of room do you want?

     Quisiera una habitación individual.   = I would like <u>a single room</u>.

a double room: una habitación doble

(3)   *¿Cuántas noches quiere quedarse?*   = How many nights do you want to stay?

     Quisiera quedarme una noche.   = I would like to stay for <u>one night</u>.

two weeks: dos semanas

For other times, see p.3.

(4)   *¿Cuándo quiere quedarse?*   = When would you like to stay?

     Quisiera quedarme desde el cinco de julio hasta el diez de julio.

       = I would like to stay from <u>the fifth of July</u> until <u>the tenth of July</u>.

For other dates, see p.4.

(5)   *¿Cuánto cuesta?*   = How much is that?

Learn the questions as well as the answers

This page is tricky, but not impossible. Make sure you come up with answers that are different to the examples given above. This will also come in useful for things like camping.

Camping

Obviously you might not want to stay in a hotel — maybe you'd <u>prefer</u> to go <u>camping</u> instead.

At the campsite — En el camping

Learn this important <u>camping</u> vocabulary.

el saco de dormir
sleeping bag

la parcela
pitch

el agua potable
drinking water

la caravana
caravan

la tienda
tent

Booking into a **campsite** — ask for "**una parcela**"

Use these phrases to <u>book into a campsite</u>.

(1)   *¿Tiene una parcela libre?*   = Do you have a free pitch?

(2)   *¿Qué tipo de parcela quiere?*   = What type of pitch do you want?

Quisiera una parcela para una tienda.   = I would like a pitch for <u>a tent</u>.

> *a caravan:* una caravana

To say <u>when</u> and <u>how long</u> you're <u>staying</u>, adapt the <u>sentences</u> in <u>points 3 and 4</u> on <u>p.90</u>.

Change the hotel conversation — swap "habitación" for "parcela"

If you got the hang of the hotel conversation on p.90, asking for a pitch shouldn't cause you any problems. The camping vocab will be really handy if you need a sleeping bag, too.

Practice Questions

Track 15   Listening Questions

1   Listen to this radio weather forecast for the different parts of Spain.
Write down North, East, West and South, then write the letter(s) to show the
weather in each area. Each area may have more than one type of weather.

A it's snowing   **E** it's sunny

B it's cloudy   **F** it's hot

C it's windy   **G** it's cold

D it's stormy   **H** it's raining

Track 16

2   Listen to Señora Álvarez booking hotel rooms.
Write down whether each statement is true or false.

a)   Señora Álvarez wants to book rooms for four nights.

b)   She wants one double room and two single rooms.

c)   She wants a bath in each room.

d)   Double rooms cost 80 euros a night.

3   Copy and complete these phrases by filling in the gaps with 'hace', 'está' or 'hay'.

a)   .... sol   c)   .... calor   e)   .... tormenta

b)   .... lloviendo   d)   .... nevando   f)   .... nublado

4   Copy and complete these sentences by filling in the correct season from the box.

a)   Julio es un mes en ....

b)   Diciembre es un mes en ....

c)   Octubre es un mes en ....

d)   Abril es un mes en ....

> la primavera
> el invierno
> el otoño
> el verano

5   Write out these words in Spanish.

a) caravan   b) sleeping bag   c) drinking water   d) tent   e) pitch

Practice Questions

6   Read what Marisol has written about her holidays,
then answer the questions below in English.

> ¡Hola! Normalmente voy de vacaciones al sur de Portugal.
> Voy en coche con mi madre, mi padrastro y mi hermano. Paso
> dos semanas en un hotel. Hay una piscina pero prefiero nadar
> en el mar. Hace mucho calor y me gusta leer en la playa.

a)   Where does she normally go?

b)   Who does she go with?

c)   How does she get there?

d)   How long does she go for?

e)   Where does she stay?

f)   What is the weather like?

7   Write out in Spanish how you would describe these rooms.
I've done the first one for you.

a)   +

Una habitación individual con ducha.

c)   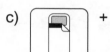 +

b)   +

d)   +

8   Write these sentences in Spanish.

a)   Do you have a free pitch?

b)   I would like a pitch for a caravan.

c)   I would like a pitch for a tent.

d)   I would like to stay for 5 nights.

9   Who says what? Read the letters, then for each statement write Peter or Emma.

> Quisiera reservar una habitación
> individual con baño. Me quedo una
> semana desde el once hasta el
> dieciocho de julio. Peter

> Quisiera reservar una parcela para
> una tienda. Me quedo dos
> semanas, desde el seis hasta el
> veinte de agosto. Emma

a)   I'm going camping.

b)   I'm staying for one week.

c)   I want to be able to have a bath.

d)   I'm going in August.

Countries

You don't need to know which country's which — just what the <u>country</u> is called in <u>Spanish</u>.

Countries — **Los países** ["el país" = country]

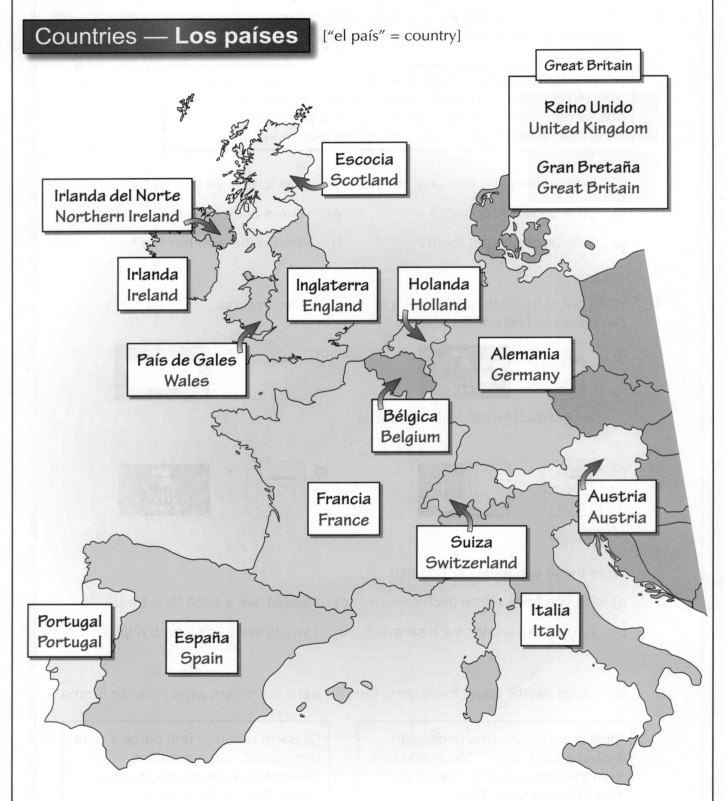

Great Britain

Reino Unido
United Kingdom

Gran Bretaña
Great Britain

Escocia
Scotland

Irlanda del Norte
Northern Ireland

Irlanda
Ireland

Inglaterra
England

Holanda
Holland

Alemania
Germany

País de Gales
Wales

Bélgica
Belgium

Austria
Austria

Francia
France

Suiza
Switzerland

Portugal
Portugal

España
Spain

Italia
Italy

Learn the countries so you can answer questions about holidays

Countries are really useful to learn — your teacher might ask you about your last holiday or your dream holiday. If you don't know all the countries on this page, it might get a bit tricky.

Nationalities

People always want to know <u>where you're from</u>. I'd be surprised if it wasn't one of the <u>first</u> <u>questions</u> you're asked when you meet someone new, so make sure you can <u>answer</u> it.

Tell people **where you live**

> *¿Dónde vives?* = Where do you live?

This is how you'd <u>reply</u> and say <u>where you live</u>:

Vivo en + COUNTRY

Vivo en `Irlanda del Norte`.

= I live in <u>Northern Ireland</u>.

Vivo en `Escocia`.

= I live in <u>Scotland</u>.

Vivo en `Inglaterra`.

= I live in <u>England</u>.

Vivo en `País de Gales`.

= I live in <u>Wales</u>.

Understand **where other people live**

If someone tells you <u>where they live</u>, you need to be able to <u>understand</u> them:

> *Vivo en* `España`. = I live in <u>Spain</u>.

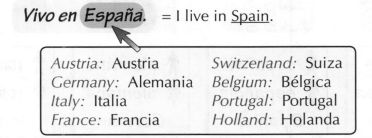

Austria: Austria	*Switzerland:* Suiza
Germany: Alemania	*Belgium:* Bélgica
Italy: Italia	*Portugal:* Portugal
France: Francia	*Holland:* Holanda

You'll understand where people are from if you know your countries

It might be obvious, but the key to understanding where people are from is knowing the countries really well. If you don't know the countries yet, go back and revise them on p.94.

Nationalities

It's always handy to be able to say <u>your nationality</u>, too.

Talk about your **nationality**

Nationality words <u>change</u> depending on whether you're <u>male</u> or <u>female</u>. If you're <u>female</u>, you <u>don't</u> need an accent on the final "<u>e</u>", but you do need to <u>add</u> an "<u>a</u>" at the <u>end</u>.

Soy + NATIONALITY

You don't need a capital letter for nationalities in Spanish.

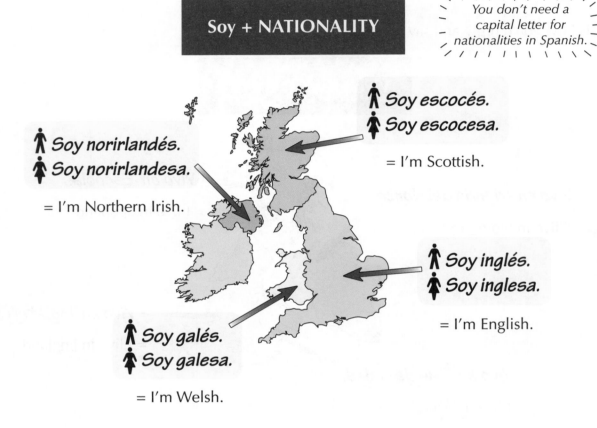

♦ *Soy norirlandés.*
♦ *Soy norirlandesa.*

= I'm Northern Irish.

♦ *Soy escocés.*
♦ *Soy escocesa.*

= I'm Scottish.

♦ *Soy inglés.*
♦ *Soy inglesa.*

= I'm English.

♦ *Soy galés.*
♦ *Soy galesa.*

= I'm Welsh.

Some **other nationalities**

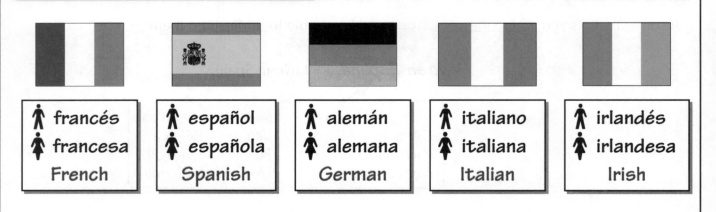

♦ francés	♦ español	♦ alemán	♦ italiano	♦ irlandés
♦ francesa	♦ española	♦ alemana	♦ italiana	♦ irlandesa
French	Spanish	German	Italian	Irish

Nationalities don't have a capital letter in Spanish

Learn all these nationalities — they're bound to come up in class. Just don't forget that with certain nationalities, you need to remove the accent for the feminine version and add an "a".

Practice Questions

1   Where do these people live? Write the answer in English.

a) Vivo en Holanda.   b) Vivo en Alemania.   c) Vivo en Irlanda.   d) Vivo en Suiza.   e) Vivo en Bélgica.

2   Write down what these people would say about themselves in Spanish.
Example: "Fabienne lives in France." *Vivo en Francia.*

    a)   Marco lives in Italy.   c)   Anabel lives in Spain.

    b)   Pablo lives in Portugal.   d)   Hans lives in Austria.

3   Write down the male and female versions for these nationalities in Spanish.

    a)   English   c)   Scottish

    b)   Northern Irish   d)   Welsh

4   Imagine that you are each of these people. Write down how you would
describe your nationality in Spanish.
Example: "Adam — German" *Soy alemán.*

    a)   Chloe — English   d)   David — Spanish

    b)   Patrick — Irish   e)   Anna — Italian

    c)   Adèle — French   f)   Gareth — Welsh

5   Read this email. Write 'true' or 'false' for each statement.

> ¡Hola! Vivo en la capital de España. Soy española. Mi madre es irlandesa
> y mi padre es español. Mi mejor amiga se llama Beth. Es escocesa.
> Mi profesor de biología es galés y mi profesora de geografía es alemana.

The person who wrote this...

    a)   ...is a boy.   d)   ...has a best friend who's French.

    b)   ...lives in Spain.   e)   ...has a biology teacher who's Welsh.

    c)   ...has a mother who's Irish.   f)   ...has a geography teacher who's English.

Summary Questions

There was a lot to get your head around in that section so here's a page of questions so you can make sure you've learnt everything. If you don't know the answers to any of the questions, flick back through the section, find the answers and do the questions again.

1) Your Spanish friend, Javier, wants to know what the weather is like in the UK.
   Say that it is cold and raining.

2) Javier says that it's hot and sunny. How would he say that in Spanish?

3) Write down all four seasons in Spanish.

4) You're telling Eva about where you normally go on holiday. Say this in Spanish:
   "Normally I go to Italy. I go with my mother and my sister.
   I spend one week there. I stay in a hotel. I go swimming."

5) How would you say these in Spanish? a) youth hostel   b) campsite

6) What are these in Spanish?
   a) tent   b) drinking water   c) pitch   d) caravan   e) sleeping bag

7) Write these down in Spanish:
   a) key   c) single room   e) double room
   b) room with a bath   d) dining room   f) toilets

8) You walk into a hotel in Barcelona. Ask if they have any rooms free.

9) Tell them you'd like a single room with a balcony.

10) Say you want to stay for 3 nights from 5th March to 8th March.
    Ask how much it costs.

11) You arrive at a campsite in Peru. In Spanish, ask if they have a free pitch.

12) Tell them you'd like a pitch for a tent for two weeks.

13) Say you want to stay from the 6th September until the 13th September.

14) Write down all four countries in the UK.

15) What's the Spanish for these?
    a) France   b) Holland   c) Italy   d) Ireland   e) Austria   f) Spain

16) What are these in English?
    a) Suiza   b) Alemania   c) Portugal   d) Bélgica

17) Write down in Spanish where you live and your nationality.

18) Write down in Spanish the <u>nationalities</u> that go with these places:
    a) France   b) Spain   c) Italy   d) Germany   e) Ireland   f) Scotland   g) Wales

Opinions

Learn these phrases well, and you'll be able to <u>give an opinion</u> on just about <u>anything</u>.

I like — Me gusta

"<u>Me gusta</u>" is used with <u>singular nouns</u> and <u>verbs</u>. For <u>plural nouns</u>, it becomes "<u>me gustan</u>".
If you use "me gusta" with <u>a noun</u>, you need to use "<u>el/la/los/las</u>" (see p.105).

Me gusta el tenis.   = I like <u>tennis</u>.   **Me gustan los deportes.**   = I like <u>sports</u>.

You can also use these <u>other phrases</u> to say you like something.

Me encanta nadar.   = I love <u>to swim</u>.   **Me encantan los libros.**   = I love <u>books</u>.

Use the infinitive of the verb after "me gusta" or "me encanta" (see p.120).

*"Me encanta" becomes "me encanta**n**" for plurals.*

Me gusta mucho el dibujo.   = I like <u>art</u> a lot.

You would use "me gustan" here if you were talking about a plural.

I don't like — No me gusta

Use "<u>no me gusta</u>" for verbs and singular nouns, and "<u>no me gustan</u>" for plural nouns.

No me gusta el rugby.   **No me gustan los plátanos.**

= I don't like <u>rugby</u>.   = I don't like <u>bananas</u>.

Here are some <u>other phrases</u> to say you don't like something.

No me gusta nada leer.   = I don't like <u>to read</u> at all.

*For plural nouns, this changes to "no me gusta**n** nada..."*

Odio los guisantes.   = I hate <u>peas</u>.

"Odio" doesn't change for plural nouns.

Always speak up about your likes and dislikes

Don't be shy about giving your opinions in Spanish. Whether you're doing speaking practice
or a writing exercise, opinions nearly always bag you extra marks in languages. So go for it.

Opinions

Even better than giving an opinion in Spanish is explaining <u>why</u> you feel that way.

Explain your opinion

Use the word "<u>porque</u>" (because) to give more <u>detail</u> about your opinions.

porque es = because it is   **porque son** = because they are

Then add in any of these <u>describing words</u> (adjectives).
Remember, the adjective <u>agrees</u> with whatever you're <u>describing</u> (see p.111).

SOME COMMON ADJECTIVES

awful:	horrible	*difficult:*	difícil	*great:*	estupendo/a
bad:	malo/a	*easy:*	fácil	*interesting:*	interesante
beautiful, lovely:	precioso/a	*fantastic:*	fantástico/a	*nice, kind:*	agradable
boring:	aburrido/a	*fun:*	divertido/a	*nice (people only):*	simpático/a
brilliant:	genial	*good:*	bueno/a	*strange:*	raro/a

Put together **whole sentences**

This is how you string all the opinion parts <u>together</u>.

verb   a noun or the infinitive   "porque es/son"   a describing word

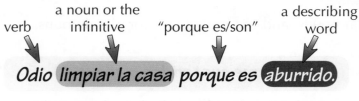

Odio limpiar la casa *porque es* aburrido.

= I hate <u>to clean the house</u> because it is <u>boring</u>.

The adjective "precioso" changes to agree with the plural. See p.111.

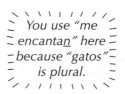

You use "me encanta<u>n</u>" here because "gatos" is plural.

Me encantan los gatos *porque son* preciosos.

= I love <u>cats</u> because they're <u>beautiful</u>.

Me gusta mucho la química *porque es* fácil.

= I like <u>chemistry</u> a lot because it's <u>easy</u>.

You can always find more adjectives in the dictionary

Just remember to make your adjective agree with your noun — you might need to change it if your noun is feminine or plural. Then go ahead and give lots of brilliant opinions in Spanish.

Asking Questions

You won't get very far in Spain if you can't ask any <u>questions</u>. That's where this page comes in.

Use ¿ and ? and your **tone of voice**

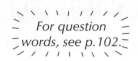

For question words, see p.102.

<u>Question marks</u> and <u>tone of voice</u> show that you're asking a question, even if you're not using a <u>question word</u>.

1) In Spanish, you can turn a <u>statement</u> into a <u>question</u> by using a pair of <u>question marks</u>. The upside down one goes at the <u>start</u> of the question and the normal one goes at the <u>end</u>.

2) Make your <u>voice</u> go <u>up</u> at the end to show that you're asking a <u>question</u>.

STATEMENT   **QUESTION**

Te gusta la playa.

= You like the beach.

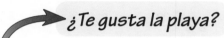

Upside down question mark.

¿Te gusta la playa?

= Do you like the beach?
  Literally: "You like the beach?"

Quiere un bocadillo.

= He wants a sandwich.

¿Quiere un bocadillo?

= Does he want a sandwich?
  Literally: "He wants a sandwich?"

Vas al instituto en autobús.

= You go to school by bus.

¿Vas al instituto en autobús?

= Do you go to school by bus?
  Literally: "You go to school by bus?"

Hay un tren para Girona.

= There is a train to Girona.

¿Hay un tren para Girona?

= Is there a train to Girona?
  Literally: "There is a train to Girona?"

Write down as many questions in Spanish as you can

Upside down question marks might look funny to us, but without them you can't ask a thing in Spanish. The more you practise using them, the more normal they'll start to look.

Asking Questions

In most cases, if you want to ask a question, you're going to need a <u>question word</u>.

Learn these **question words**

These words are short but <u>important</u>. You'll have to learn them all (and their <u>accents</u> too).

¿cuánto? = how much?   *¿cuándo?* = when?

¿cuál? = which?   *¿dónde?* = where?   *¿quién?* = who?

¿qué? = what?   *¿cómo?* = how?

Make up some **questions**

When asking questions, remember these two points:
1) Question words usually come <u>before</u> the verb in a question.
2) You always need <u>both question marks</u>.

¿Cuándo cenan? = When do they have dinner?

¿Cuál te gusta? = Which do you like?

¿Qué haces los sábados? = What do you do on Saturdays?

¿Cómo te llamas? = What are you called?

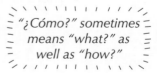
"¿Cómo?" sometimes means "what?" as well as "how?"

Accents are really important with question words

For example, "¿cómo?" with an accent means "how?". But "¿como?" <u>without</u> an accent means "I eat?". That's not really a mistake you want to make if you're after good marks in Spanish.

Practice Questions

1   Use the key to write opinions in Spanish about the school subjects below.

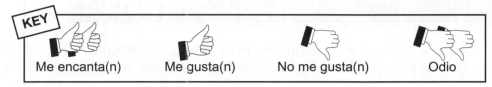

KEY — Me encanta(n)   Me gusta(n)   No me gusta(n)   Odio

For example:

el español  *Me encanta el español.*

a)   el dibujo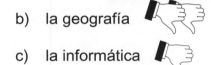

d)   las ciencias

b)   la geografía

e)   las matemáticas

c)   la informática

f)   la historia

2   Write out these sentences in Spanish.

a)   I don't like chess because it's difficult.

b)   I like listening to the radio because it's interesting.

c)   I hate washing the car because it's awful.

d)   I love sports because they're fun.

3   What do the following questions mean in English?

a)   ¿Cuándo es tu cumpleaños?

d)   ¿Cuánto cuesta una limonada?

b)   ¿Dónde vive Sandra?

e)   ¿A qué hora comes?

c)   ¿Cómo está tu madre?

f)   ¿Quién es Alexis?

4   Read these answers, then write down what the question would be in Spanish.
Choose one of the question words in the box to start each question.

For example: Tengo trece años.   *¿Cuántos años tienes?*

~~cuántos~~	dónde	cuándo	qué	cómo	cuánto	cuál

a)   Vivo en Valencia.

d)   Mi número de teléfono es el 21 45 83.

b)   El libro cuesta cinco euros.

e)   El tren sale a las cuatro y media.

c)   Voy al instituto en autobús.

f)   En mi dormitorio hay una cama.

Words for People and Objects

Use this page to learn the differences between <u>masculine</u>, <u>feminine</u>, <u>singular</u> and <u>plural</u> words.

Every Spanish noun is **masculine** or **feminine**

You can tell if a word is masculine or feminine by its <u>article</u>. Words that have "<u>el</u>" or "<u>un</u>" before them are <u>masculine</u>. Words that have "<u>la</u>" or "<u>una</u>" before them are <u>feminine</u>. See p.105-106.

> **THE GOLDEN RULE**
> Each time you learn a word, learn the
> "el" or "la" to go with it. Don't think
> "gato = cat", think "<u>el</u> gato = cat".

Making nouns **plural**

Here's how to turn <u>singular nouns</u> into <u>plural nouns</u> in Spanish.

A plural noun simply means more than one of something.

1) If the noun ends in a <u>vowel</u>, you add "<u>s</u>".

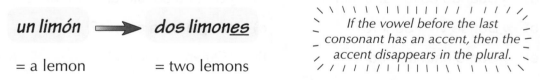

una pera ➡ **dos pera<u>s</u>**	**un tomate** ➡ **dos tomate<u>s</u>**
= a pear = two pears	= a tomato = two tomatoes

2) If a noun ends in a <u>consonant</u>, you usually add "<u>es</u>".

un limón ➡ **dos limon<u>es</u>**

If the vowel before the last consonant has an accent, then the accent disappears in the plural.

= a lemon   = two lemons

3) If a noun ends in "<u>z</u>", you have to change the "<u>z</u>" to a "<u>c</u>" and add "<u>es</u>".

un lápiz ➡ **dos lápi<u>ces</u>**

The <u>Golden Rule</u> works here as well. Each time you learn a new word, learn how to make it plural.

= a pencil   = two pencils

Always learn whether a word is masculine or feminine

It may take a bit of getting used to because this is so different to English. Learn whether a word is masculine or feminine, and how to say more than one of something right from the start.

How to Say 'The'

These words might be <u>small</u>, but you won't get far in Spanish without them.
You'll use them <u>all the time</u> so it's worth getting to grips with them <u>ASAP</u>.

The — el, la, los, las

The Spanish word for "<u>the</u>" changes depending on whether a word is <u>masculine</u>, <u>feminine</u>, <u>singular</u> or <u>plural</u>. The table below shows which word for "<u>the</u>" to use when.

THE	MASCULINE	FEMININE
SINGULAR	EL	LA
PLURAL	LOS	LAS

Grammar Fans: these are called "<u>Definite Articles</u>".

el coche = <u>the</u> car ➡ **los** coches = <u>the</u> cars

la casa = <u>the</u> house ➡ **las** casas = <u>the</u> houses

One exception is "el agua" (water). "Agua" is feminine even though it goes with "el".

How to say "**to the**" and "**of the**"

You can't say "<u>a el</u>" ("<u>to the</u>") or "<u>de el</u>" ("<u>of the</u>" or "<u>from the</u>") in Spanish.
Instead you say "<u>al</u>" (a + el) and "<u>del</u>" (de + el) before a <u>masculine noun</u>.

a + el = al

de + el = del

Vamos **al** *parque.*

= We go <u>to the</u> park.

El libro **del** *profesor.*

= The teacher's book.

Literally, "The book <u>of the</u> teacher."

Voy **al** *camping.*

= I go <u>to the</u> campsite.

Soy **del** *Reino Unido.*

= I'm <u>from the</u> UK.

Remember, you say "a la" and "de la" with feminine nouns.

Learn the four words for "the" and don't forget "al" and "del"

The reason "a + el" and "de + el" change is because "al" and "del" are easier to say. It's not so easy to remember this rule when you're writing though, so always check your written work.

How to Say 'A'

This page focuses on <u>four little words</u>: two words for "<u>a</u>" and two words for "<u>some</u>".

How to say "a" — **un, una**

Just like the word for "<u>the</u>", the word for "<u>a</u>" changes too.
When you make "<u>un</u>" or "<u>una</u>" plural, they mean "<u>some</u>".

> Grammar Fans:
> these are called
> "<u>Indefinite Articles</u>".

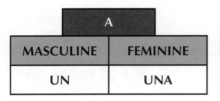

A	
MASCULINE	**FEMININE**
UN	UNA

SOME	
MASCULINE	**FEMININE**
UNOS	UNAS

*Tengo **un** caballo.* = I have <u>a</u> horse.

*Tengo **unos** caballos.* = I have <u>some</u> horses.

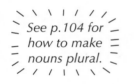

See p.104 for
how to make
nouns plural.

*Tengo **una** manzana.* = I have <u>an</u> apple

*Tengo **unas** manzanas.* = I have <u>some</u> apples.

When not to use **un** and **una**

You don't always use the Spanish word for "<u>a</u>" when you would use it in English.
For example, you <u>leave it out</u>:

1) After the verb "<u>ser</u>" for <u>someone's occupation</u>:

Es médica. = She's a doctor.

2) In <u>negative sentences</u>:

> In Spanish, there isn't a
> special word for "any".

No tengo animales en casa. = I don't have any pets.

This is why you need to know if a noun is masculine or feminine

Take this short list of vocab and go through it, checking you know how to put each word with "un" or "una" and "unos" or "unas": "el perro", "el tomate", "la camisa", "la silla", "el libro".

I, You, He, She

<u>Pronouns</u> are words such as "<u>he</u>", "<u>she</u>" and "<u>they</u>" which save you from repeating <u>nouns</u>.

Oscar wants to be a doctor so he studies really hard.

"He" is the pronoun. It means you don't have to use "Oscar" again.

I, you, he, she — Yo, tú, él, ella

These are the <u>subject pronouns</u> ("<u>I</u>", "<u>he</u>", "<u>they</u>") in Spanish.

Grammar Fans: these are called "<u>Subject Pronouns</u>".

I =	*yo*	*nosotros/as*	= we
you (singular) =	*tú*	*vosotros/as*	= you (plural)
he =	*él*	*ellos*	= they (boys + mixed)
she =	*ella*	*ellas*	= they (girls only)

The "-as" endings are for groups of girls only.
The "-os" endings can be for boys or a mixed group.

Spanish uses **subject pronouns** differently

1) <u>Subject pronouns</u> are not as <u>common</u> in Spanish as they are in English.

2) They're often <u>optional</u>, because the <u>verb ending</u> can tell you <u>who</u> is <u>doing the action</u>.

3) They're usually used for <u>emphasis</u>, or to <u>make it clear</u> who you're talking about.

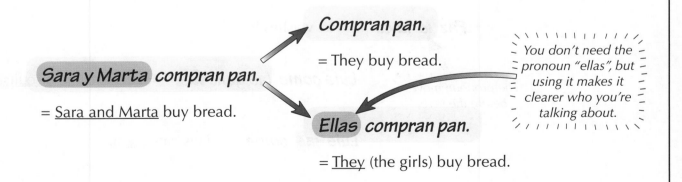

Compran pan.

= They buy bread.

Sara y Marta compran pan.

= <u>Sara and Marta</u> buy bread.

Ellas compran pan.

= <u>They</u> (the girls) buy bread.

You don't need the pronoun "ellas", but using it makes it clearer who you're talking about.

Make sure you learn these subject pronouns

As well as emphasising who's doing the action, subject pronouns can be the only way to make it clear who's doing what. If you don't learn them, you risk being caught in a right muddle.

Me, You, Him, Her

A <u>direct object pronoun</u> replaces <u>a noun</u> that is having an action <u>done to it</u>.
Look at the example below in English.

Helen plays *the guitar.* ➡ **Helen plays** <u>*it.*</u>

*"The guitar" is the noun
having the action done to it.*

*"It" is a a direct object pronoun which
can replace the word "guitar".*

Me, you, him — **Me, te, lo**

These are the <u>direct object pronouns</u> in Spanish:

me =	*me*	*nos*	= us
you (singular) =	*te*	*os*	= you (plural)
him / it =	*lo*	*los*	= them (masculine)
her / it =	*la*	*las*	= them (feminine)

Using direct object pronouns

When you want to use a <u>direct object pronoun</u>, follow this <u>simple rule</u>:
<u>replace the noun</u> with a <u>direct object pronoun</u> then move it <u>before the verb</u>.

Paz lava *el perro.* = Paz washes <u>the dog</u>.

Paz *lo* **lava.** = Paz washes <u>it</u>.

*The pronoun moves
before the verb.*

Luis come *las galletas.* = Luis eats <u>the biscuits</u>.

Luis *las* **come.** = Luis eats <u>them</u>.

There are two key things to learn on this page

Firstly, you need to know <u>what</u> all the direct object pronouns are, and secondly, <u>where</u> they go in a sentence. Write a phrase for each pronoun to check that you've mastered both points.

Practice Questions

1 Write out the following words as plurals. The first one has been done for you.

a) una revista → dos _revistas_

b) una pera → dos ....

c) una granja → dos ....

d) un armario → dos ....

e) una calle → dos ....

f) una bicicleta → dos ....

g) un tomate → dos ....

h) una clase → dos ....

i) un vestido → dos ....

j) un parque → dos ....

2 Copy out these sentences, writing each word in brackets in its plural form.

a) Tengo cuatro [hermana].

b) Miguel come muchos [plátano].

c) Mis primos son [albañil].

d) En mi casa hay seis [habitación].

e) En la pastelería hay muchos [pastel].

f) En nuestro salón tenemos dos [sillón].

If you're struggling with plurals, go back to p.104 for another look.

3 Rewrite these Spanish words with 'el', 'la', 'los' or 'las'.

a) una tortuga

b) unas revistas

c) un médico

d) unas corbatas

e) un bocadillo

f) una tirita

g) unos actores

h) un restaurante

i) unas reglas

j) una trompeta

4 Write out these sentences using the correct option from the brackets.

a) El banco está enfrente [del / de la] supermercado.

b) El cine está al lado [del / de la] farmacia.

c) Para ir [al / a la] banco, tome la primera calle [al / a la] derecha.

d) La estación está [al / a la] final [del / de la] calle.

e) Para ir [al / a la] playa, tome la segunda calle [al / a la] izquierda.

Practice Questions

5   Write out these English sentences in Spanish.

a)   I don't have any pets.

b)   I don't have any brothers.

c)   I don't have any pens.

d)   I don't have any money.

6   Copy and complete the table using the Spanish subject pronouns from the box.

HINT: all of these 'you's are in the familiar form.

she	you (singular)	I	we	they (feminine)	you (plural)	he	they (masculine)

nosotros	yo	él	ellos	vosotros	tú	ella	ellas

7   Complete each sentence using the correct direct object pronoun from the box.

DIRECT OBJECT PRONOUNS			
me	te	nos	os

a)   My grandmother visits <u>us</u>.   →   Mi abuela .... visita.

b)   Janice and Deborah see <u>me</u>.   →   Janice y Deborah .... ven.

c)   I know <u>you</u> (singular).   →   .... conozco.

d)   I'm looking at <u>you</u> (plural).   →   .... miro.

8   Complete each sentence using the correct direct object pronoun from the box.

DIRECT OBJECT PRONOUNS			
lo	la	los	las

a)   Mi madre limpia <u>la casa</u>.   →   Mi madre .... limpia.

b)   Ellos lavan <u>los coches</u>.   →   Ellos .... lavan.

c)   Rafael compra <u>unas manzanas</u>.   →   Rafael .... compra.

d)   Natalia quiere <u>unos zapatos</u>.   →   Natalia .... quiere.

e)   Nosotros bebemos <u>el zumo</u>.   →   Nosotros .... bebemos.

Words to Describe Things

Adjectives in Spanish work differently to English. They change to match the noun they go with.

Adjectives "agree" with what they're describing

This example shows you how "blanco" changes to agree with different nouns.

1) If the adjective ends in an "o" in its masculine singular form, add an "s" to make it plural.

el coche blanco ➡ *los coches blanco<u>s</u>*

= the white car   = the white cars

> Grammar Fans:
> these are called
> "Adjectives".

2) Change the "o" to an "a" for a feminine singular noun. Add an "s" for feminine plurals.

la casa blanc<u>a</u> ➡ *las casas blanc<u>as</u>*

= the white house   = the white houses

3) If an adjective ends in "e", it stays the same for masculine and feminine words.
You just add an "s" to the adjectives when the noun is plural.

el coche grande = the big car ➡ *los coches grande<u>s</u>* = the big cars

la casa grande = the big house ➡ *las casas grande<u>s</u>* = the big houses

Most describing words go after the noun

In English, the describing word goes in front of the noun.
We say "the hot soup" not "the soup hot". But not in Spanish.

Quiero un bocadillo grande.   *Tienen dos bicicletas* nuevas.

= I want a <u>big</u> sandwich.   = They have two <u>new</u> bikes.
Literally, "I want a sandwich big."   *Literally, "They have two bikes new."*

There's a lot of information here, so take your time on this page

Not only do you have to learn how to form the four different forms (masculine, feminine, singular and plural) of the adjective, but you have to remember where it goes in the sentence.

Making Comparisons

Being able to <u>compare</u> things can be pretty useful.

"Más' is "more"

> Grammar Fans: "More" and "less" words are "<u>Comparatives</u>". "The most" and "the least" words are "<u>Superlatives</u>".

In Spanish you can't say "<u>bigger</u>" or "<u>biggest</u>". You have to say "<u>more big</u>" or "<u>the most big</u>".

Mi sombrero es grande.   = My hat is big.

Mi sombrero es **más** *grande.*   = My hat is bigger.
Literally: my hat is <u>more</u> big.

Mi sombrero es **el más** *grande.*   = My hat is the biggest.
Literally: my hat is <u>the most</u> big.

"<u>El más</u>" becomes "<u>la más</u>" if a noun is <u>feminine singular</u> and "<u>los/las más</u>" if it's <u>plural</u>.

Esta clase es **la más** *aburrida.*   = This class is <u>the most</u> boring.

"Menos" is "less"

To say that something is "<u>less</u>" something, use the word "<u>menos</u>":

Raúl es perezoso.   = Raúl is lazy.

Raúl es **menos** *perezoso.*   = Raúl is <u>less</u> lazy.

Raúl es **el menos** *perezoso.*   = Raúl is <u>the least</u> lazy.

"<u>El menos</u>" becomes "<u>la menos</u>" if a noun is <u>feminine singular</u> and "<u>los/las menos</u>" if it's <u>plural</u>.

Mis gatos son **los menos** *gordos.*   = My cats are <u>the least</u> fat.

Practise forming lots of comparison phrases

In comparison phrases, always check if your noun is masculine or feminine, and if it's a plural or not. Then make sure that both the "el/la/los/las" <u>and</u> the adjective agree with the noun.

Making Comparisons

This page on comparisons might be a little trickier, but it's still "need-to-know" stuff.

These comparing words are irregular

Some of the most common comparison words don't follow the "el más/el menos" pattern. These are the odd ones out. They're important ones, so make sure you learn them well.

GOOD, BETTER, BEST

good = *bueno*
better = *mejor*
the best = *el mejor*

BAD, WORSE, WORST

bad = *malo*
worse = *peor*
the worst = *el peor*

OLD, OLDER, OLDEST

old = *viejo*
older = *mayor*
the oldest = *el mayor*

YOUNG, YOUNGER, YOUNGEST

young = *joven*
younger = *menor*
the youngest = *el menor*

Learn these three ways to compare things

Use these handy phrases to compare things.

más ... que
= more ... than

menos ... que
= less ... than

tan ... como
= as ... as

Soy más alto que tú. = I am taller than you. (Literally, "I am more tall than you.")

Soy tan alto como tú. = I am as tall as you.

Comparisons will make your Spanish sound more interesting

Speaking Spanish isn't about reeling off a load of vocab — it's about being able to make interesting and useful sentences. That's why the stuff on this page is great to learn and use.

My and Your

Sometimes, grammar boils down to simply learning lots of incredibly useful little words.

How to say "my", "your", "our"

Grammar Fans: these are called "Possessive Adjectives".

1) Words like "my", "your" or "her" show that something belongs to someone.

2) In Spanish, these words have masculine, feminine, singular and plural forms.

3) Important: the possessive adjectives agree with the thing — not the person they belong to.

	masculine singular	feminine singular	masculine plural	feminine plural
my	mi	mi	mis	mis
your (singular)	tu	tu	tus	tus
his/her/its	su	su	sus	sus
our	nuestro	nuestra	nuestros	nuestras
your (plural)	vuestro	vuestra	vuestros	vuestras
their	su	su	sus	sus

Using possessive adjectives

Nuestra casa es pequeña.   = Our house is small.

Feminine singular

Vuestros padres son simpáticos.   = Your (plural) parents are nice.

Masculine plural

Tengo tus camisas y tu jersey.   = I have your shirts and your jumper.

Feminine plural   *Masculine singular*

Don't let a table full of words put you off

These words will soon seem familiar, because you'll hear them quite a lot in Spanish.
When you use them yourself, always double-check you've got the agreement right.

This and These

Here's another page of <u>little grammar words</u> you couldn't live without in Spanish.

How to say "**this**" and "**that**"

These words also <u>have to agree</u> with the nouns they go with.

> Grammar Fans: these are called
> "<u>Demonstrative Adjectives</u>".

	masculine	feminine
this	este	esta
that	ese	esa
these	estos	estas
those	esos	esas

Esta bicicleta. = <u>This</u> bike.

Ese restaurante. = <u>That</u> restaurant.

Esas sillas. = <u>Those</u> chairs.

Estos libros. = <u>These</u> books.

Using **demonstrative and possessive adjectives**

The <u>demonstrative adjectives</u> are in red and the <u>possessive adjectives</u> are in green.

Esta casa es mi casa. = <u>This</u> house is <u>my</u> house.

Ese tren es nuestro tren. = <u>That</u> train is <u>our</u> train.

Esa revista es su favorita. = <u>That</u> magazine is <u>her</u> favourite.

> "Su" could
> also mean
> "his" or "their",
> depending on
> the context.

With lots of practice, you'll nail both types of adjectives

It's easier to recognise these words than to remember them off the top of your head. Write your own sentences with demonstrative and possessive adjectives to really help them sink in.

'Por' and 'Para'

"Por" and "para" confuse nearly everyone. They can both mean "for", but in different situations. Learn the examples below to help you decide when to use "para".

Use **Para** for...

1) Saying who something is for:

   El zumo es **para** *Paula.*   = The juice is for Paula.

2) Talking about a destination:

   El avión **para** *Barcelona.*   = The plane to Barcelona.

   See p.75 for methods of transport.

3) When you want to say "to"/"in order to":

   Voy al parque **para** *jugar al fútbol.*   = I go to the park in order to play football.

4) Specific periods of time when you're talking about the future:

   Voy a ir a España **para** *una semana.*   = I am going to go to Spain for a week.

5) When you want to say "by" in time phrases:

   "Haga los deberes **para** *mañana."*   = "Do the homework by tomorrow."

   See p.135-136 for the imperative.

Learn these five examples really well

Have a go at writing your own sentences with "para", using the examples to help you. It's also great practice to try and notice where "para" is used in any Spanish writing that you read.

'Por' and 'Para'

There are other situations where you would use "por", but these are some common ones.

Use Por for...

1) Talking about parts of the day:

por la mañana   **por** la tarde   **por** la noche

= in the morning   = in the afternoon/evening   = at night

After a time, "por" changes to "de" — e.g. "son las ocho de la mañana" (it's eight o'clock in the morning).

2) When you say "through":

Voy por el mercado.   = I go through the market.

El coche pasa por el túnel.   = The car goes through the tunnel.

3) Exchanges, like prices or amounts of money:

Pago dos euros por el autobús.   = I pay two euros for the bus.

Te doy mi regla por tu lápiz.   = I'll give you my ruler for your pencil.

4) Saying "thank you for...":

Gracias por el regalo.   = Thank you for the gift.

Remember these examples to help you use "por"

Just like learning "para", the best way to learn where to use "por" is to practise using it yourself. Write your own sentences, one for each of the four points on the page.

Practice Questions

Track 17   Listening Questions

Listen to Santiago, Teresa and David comparing members of their families. Write down whether each statement is true or false.

1   a)   Santiago says that his mother is fatter than his father.

      b)   Santiago says that both his uncles are as stupid as each other.

2   a)   Teresa says that her mother is nicer than her father.

      b)   Teresa says that her brother is more intelligent than her sister.

3   a)   David says that his mother is slimmer than his sister.

      b)   David says that his brother is more fun than his sister.

4   Copy and complete the following sentences using the correct form of the adjective in brackets.

     a)   Mi casa no es muy *[grande]*.

     b)   Las sillas son *[raro]*.

     c)   Mi amiga es *[inteligente]*.

     d)   Mi hermana es *[trabajador]*.

     e)   Estos deberes son *[difícil]*.

     f)   Mis pantalones son *[verde]* y *[largo]*.

     g)   Mi primo es *[horrible]* pero mi tía es *[simpático]*.

     h)   Tengo dos lápices *[rojo]* y un bolígrafo *[negro]*.

5   Complete these sentences to translate what each person is saying into Spanish. For example:

          I'm wearing a white dress. → *Llevo un vestido blanco.*

Augustín: I like my green tortoises. → Me gustan ....

Luisa: I live in a small house. → Vivo en ....

Rodolfo: I want a big pizza. → Quiero ....

Ornella: I have some good books. → Tengo ....

Rodrigo: Let's go to the new cinema. → Vamos al ....

Practice Questions

6 Copy and complete each Spanish sentence using the correct possessive adjective: 'mi', 'tu' or 'su'. Remember that these words change for plural nouns.

a) Where are his parents?   ¿Dónde están .... padres?

b) My shoes are very comfortable.   .... zapatos son muy cómodos.

c) Are their friends here?   ¿......... amigos están aquí?

d) Your books are on her bed.   .... libros están en .... cama.

e) My uncle is your teacher.   .... tío es .... profesor.

7 Copy and complete each Spanish sentence using either 'nuestro' or 'vuestro'. Remember that these words change to match the noun.

a) Our grandmother is intelligent.   .... abuela es inteligente.

b) Your houses are nearby.   .... casas están cerca.

c) Our dogs are friendly.   .... perros son simpáticos.

d) Your cousins live with our cousins.   .... primos viven con .... primas.

8 Copy and complete these tables using the Spanish words for 'this', 'that', 'these' and 'those'.

the book	el libro
this book	
that book	*ese libro*
these books	
those books	

the shirt	la camisa
this shirt	*esta camisa*
that shirt	
these shirts	
those shirts	

9 For each sentence, write 'por' or 'para' to translate the underlined word.

a) the train <u>to</u> Barcelona

b) she left <u>in</u> the afternoon

c) the cake is <u>for</u> you

d) 3 euros <u>for</u> one ice cream

e) we went <u>through</u> the park

f) she's going <u>for</u> three days

g) thank you <u>for</u> your letter

h) I want it <u>by</u> tomorrow

i) he plays <u>in</u> the morning

j) the coach <u>to</u> London

Verbs in the Present Tense

It's time to learn how to <u>deal with verbs</u>. There are a <u>lot of endings</u> so <u>take your time</u>.

The **infinitive** means "**to + verb**"

When you look up a Spanish <u>verb</u> in a dictionary, you'll find the <u>infinitive</u>, like "<u>hablar</u>".
In Spanish, the infinitive is made of a <u>stem</u> and an <u>ending</u>.
The ending is the <u>last two letters</u> of the infinitive.

This is how to form the <u>present tense</u> in Spanish:

To find the <u>stem</u>, <u>take off</u> the <u>last two letters</u> of the <u>infinitive</u>.

(1) **Find the verb stem.**

VERB	STEM
HABLAR	HABL
COMER	COM
VIVIR	VIV

(2) **Add on the new ending.**

There are 3 types of ending: -ar, -er and -ir. You can find these new endings below and on p.121.

Endings for **-ar verbs**

These are the <u>endings</u> you need to add for <u>-ar</u> verbs:

For more on the polite "you", see p.8-10.

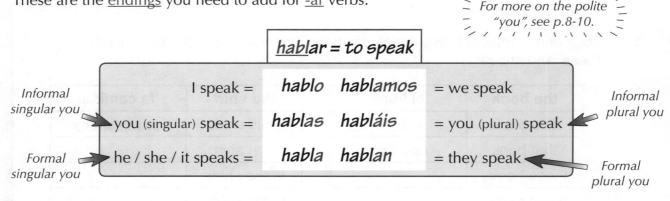

hablar = to speak

Informal singular you →	I speak =	**hablo** **hablamos**	= we speak	← *Informal plural you*
	you (singular) speak =	**hablas** **habláis**	= you (plural) speak	←
Formal singular you →	he / she / it speaks =	**habla** **hablan**	= they speak	← *Formal plural you*

Here's an example of how to form a <u>present tense</u> verb.
If you want to say "<u>I speak</u> Spanish", this is what you do:

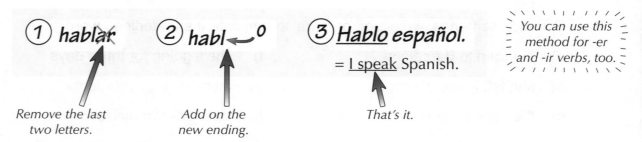

(1) *hablar*   (2) *habl* ← *o*   (3) <u>Hablo español.</u>
= <u>I speak</u> Spanish.

Remove the last two letters.   Add on the new ending.   That's it.

You can use this method for -er and -ir verbs, too.

Verbs can be tricky but you'll use them all the time

You can't write a sentence without a verb so it's really important that you learn this page well.
Learn how to get the stem and then scribble down the endings until you get them all right.

Verbs in the Present Tense

Same sort of stuff as the last page, just with <u>different verbs</u> — make a start <u>now</u>.

Endings for **-er verbs**

Use these <u>endings</u> for <u>-er</u> verbs:

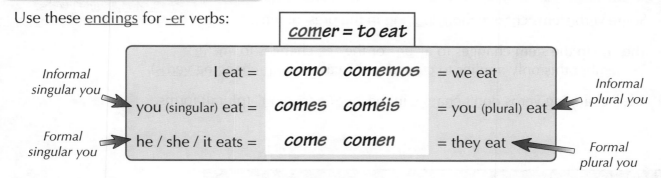

<u>com</u>er = to eat

Informal singular you	I eat =	**como** **comemos**	= we eat	*Informal plural you*
	you (singular) eat =	**comes** **coméis**	= you (plural) eat	
Formal singular you	he / she / it eats =	**come** **comen**	= they eat	*Formal plural you*

Here are some sentences which <u>use -er verbs</u>:

Everything you should need on present tense verbs is on p.120-124.

Comemos *pizza.* = <u>We eat</u> pizza.

Bebe *café con leche.* = <u>She drinks</u> coffee with milk.

Endings for **-ir verbs**

Use these <u>endings</u> for <u>-ir</u> verbs:

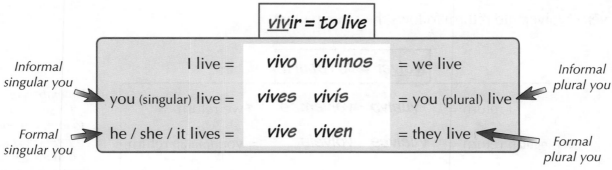

<u>viv</u>ir = to live

Informal singular you	I live =	**vivo** **vivimos**	= we live	*Informal plural you*
	you (singular) live =	**vives** **vivís**	= you (plural) live	
Formal singular you	he / she / it lives =	**vive** **viven**	= they live	*Formal plural you*

Here are some sentences which <u>use -ir verbs</u>.

Vivo *en Inglaterra.* = <u>I live</u> in England. **Escriben** *una carta.* = <u>They write</u> a letter.

Cover the endings, write them down, then check them

You need to learn all of the endings for -er and -ir verbs and then practise them. Try putting "aprender" (to learn) and "decidir" (to decide) into the present tense and see how you get on.

Verbs in the Present Tense

These <u>present tense</u> verbs are a <u>bit different</u> — their <u>stem changes</u>.

Some Spanish verbs change their stem

Grammar Fans: these are called "<u>stem-changing</u>" or "<u>radical-changing</u>" verbs.

1) Some verb stems <u>change their spelling</u> in the present tense.

2) The "<u>o</u>" in the stem changes to a "<u>ue</u>" or the "<u>e</u>" changes to an "<u>ie</u>" (remember this only applies to <u>certain verbs</u> called <u>stem-changing verbs</u>).

3) Stem-changing verbs <u>don't change</u> in the "<u>we</u>" and "<u>you</u>" (plural) forms.

When the "o" in the stem changes to "ue"

The "<u>o</u>" in "p<u>o</u>der" (to be able to) changes to "<u>ue</u>" — except for "we" and "you" plural.

	poder = to be able to		
I can =	**puedo**	**podemos**	= we can
you (singular) can =	**puedes**	**podéis**	= you (plural) can
he / she / it can =	**puede**	**pueden**	= they can

To use "poder" politely, see p.10.

No puedes nadar. = <u>You can't</u> swim.   **¿Puedo ir al baño?** = <u>Can I</u> go to the toilet?

The verb "v<u>o</u>lver" (to return) follows the same pattern:

	volver = to return		
I return =	**vuelvo**	**volvemos**	= we return
you (singular) return =	**vuelves**	**volvéis**	= you (plural) return
he / she / it returns =	**vuelve**	**vuelven**	= they return

Remember: use the "<u>he/she/it</u>" part to form the polite "<u>you</u>" (<u>singular</u>) and the "<u>they</u>" part for the polite "<u>you</u>" (<u>plural</u>) of any verb.

Vuelve a Francia cada año. = <u>He returns</u> to France each year.

Stem-changing verbs don't change for "we" and "you" plural

Stem-changing verbs are a bit trickier than regular verbs, but they're still not too bad. Remember how the stem changes, then apply this to all forms except "we" and "you" plural.

Verbs in the Present Tense

Here's a <u>different</u> type of <u>stem-changing verb</u> for you to tackle — plus two <u>examples</u>.

The "e" in the stem of these verbs changes to "ie"

The first "<u>e</u>" in "qu<u>e</u>rer" (to want) changes to "<u>ie</u>", except for "we" and "you" plural.

querer = to want		
I want =	**quiero** **queremos**	= we want
you (singular) want =	**quieres** **queréis**	= you (plural) want
he / she / it wants =	**quiere** **quieren**	= they want

Quiere *un gato.* = <u>She wants</u> a cat.

Quiero *tocar el piano.* = <u>I want</u> to play the piano.

The endings for stem-changing verbs are the same as regular verbs.

The first "<u>e</u>" in "<u>te</u>ner" (to have) also changes to "<u>ie</u>" (except for "we" and "you" plural). The "<u>I</u>" form of "<u>tener</u>" ("<u>tengo</u>") is <u>completely irregular</u>. You'll just have to learn it.

tener = to have		
I have =	**tengo** **tenemos**	= we have
you (singular) have =	**tienes** **tenéis**	= you (plural) have
he / she / it has =	**tiene** **tienen**	= they have

Tiene *dos hermanos.* = <u>He has</u> two brothers.

Tienen *un perro.* = <u>They have</u> a dog.

These two stem-changing verbs are really common

"Querer" and "tener" are used all the time so it's important that you learn them well. Practise using them in sentences, e.g. "Quiero un helado." ("I want an ice-cream.")

Irregular Verbs in the Present Tense

You'll need "to be" and "to go" all the time so it's worth memorising them now.

Some common irregular verbs

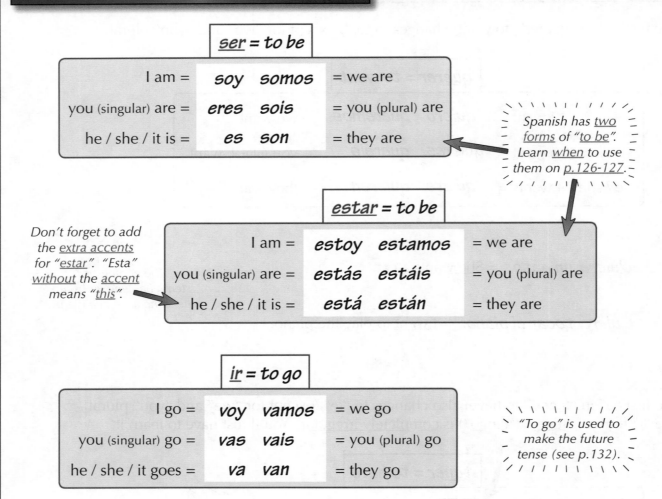

ser = to be

I am =	**soy**	**somos**	= we are
you (singular) are =	**eres**	**sois**	= you (plural) are
he / she / it is =	**es**	**son**	= they are

Spanish has two forms of "to be". Learn when to use them on p.126-127.

estar = to be

Don't forget to add the extra accents for "estar". "Esta" without the accent means "this".

I am =	**estoy**	**estamos**	= we are
you (singular) are =	**estás**	**estáis**	= you (plural) are
he / she / it is =	**está**	**están**	= they are

ir = to go

I go =	**voy**	**vamos**	= we go
you (singular) go =	**vas**	**vais**	= you (plural) go
he / she / it goes =	**va**	**van**	= they go

"To go" is used to make the future tense (see p.132).

There is = **hay**, it is = **es**

"There is" and "it is" are quite similar in English. Here's how to say them in Spanish.

1) To say "there is" or "there are" in Spanish, you say "hay" (pronounce it like "eye").

> **Hay un armario en mi dormitorio.** = There is a wardrobe in my bedroom.

2) To say "it is" in Spanish, use "es" (from the verb "ser").

> **Me gusta el libro porque es interesante.** = I like the book because it is interesting.

Remember to add the extra accents for "estar"

Irregular verbs are very common so you need to learn them. Take your time and go through them one at a time. When you're happy you know a verb inside out, move on to the next one.

Practice Questions

1   Put each of these Spanish verbs in the correct form of the present tense.

  a)   Nosotros *[cantar]*   d)   Ella *[aprender]*   g)   Yo *[beber]*

  b)   Yo *[asistir]*   e)   Vosotros *[decidir]*   h)   Nosotros *[subir]*

  c)   Él *[correr]*   f)   Tú *[ayudar]*   i)   Ellos *[preparar]*

2   Choose the correct form of 'querer' from the box to fill in the gaps in these sentences. Use each one only once.

  a)   Él .... comer patatas.

  b)   Ellos .... comer pizza.

  c)   Yo .... comer ensalada.

  d)   ¿Tú .... comer pescado?

  e)   Nosotros .... comer pasta.

  f)   Vosotros .... comer mariscos.

> *quieren*
> *queréis*
> *quiere*
> *queremos*
> *quiero*
> *quieres*

3   Write the correct form of 'tener' in the present tense.

  a)   I have   c)   You (singular) have   e)   He has

  b)   They have   d)   You (plural) have   f)   We have

4   Copy and complete these sentences by putting the irregular verb in brackets in the correct form of the present tense.

  a)   Yo *[estar]* en Madrid.   e)   Tú *[ser]* alto.

  b)   Olivia *[ser]* profesora.   f)   Yo *[ir]* a la piscina.

  c)   Iago y Nacho *[ir]* al cine.   g)   Ellos *[ser]* españoles.

  d)   Jorge *[estar]* muy contento.   h)   Ana y yo *[estar]* en el parque.

5   Copy and complete these sentences by filling in the gaps with either 'hay' or 'es'.

  a)   En mi estuche .... un lápiz que .... gris.

  b)   Mi dormitorio .... grande pero la cocina .... pequeña.

  c)   En mi dormitorio .... una cama y una mesa, pero no .... televisión.

  d)   La historia .... muy aburrida pero el inglés .... muy interesante.

  e)   .... muchos museos en París porque .... la capital de Francia.

'Ser' and 'Estar'

<u>Two</u> Spanish verbs for "<u>to be</u>" — wow. Here are some tips on how to use them <u>correctly</u>.

Ser and estar both mean "to be"

"<u>Ser</u>" and "<u>estar</u>" both mean "<u>to be</u>" in Spanish, but they're used <u>differently</u> — you <u>can't</u> just use whichever one you prefer. It can be <u>tricky</u> to know which one to use when, but here are a few <u>rules</u> to help, starting with "ser".

Use **ser** for things that **don't change**

"<u>Ser</u>" is for talking about <u>permanent</u> things:

For more <u>nationalities</u>, see p.96.

1) <u>Nationalities</u>:

Soy inglés. = <u>I am</u> English.   **Son francesas.** = <u>They are</u> French.

2) <u>Family relationships</u>:

Ese hombre es mi padre. = That man <u>is</u> my father.

See p.15 for more <u>family relationships</u> and p.39 for more <u>jobs</u>.

3) <u>Jobs</u>:

Mi hermano es médico. = My brother <u>is</u> a doctor.   **Soy actor.** = <u>I am</u> an actor.

4) <u>Physical characteristics</u>:

Su camiseta es verde. = Her T-shirt <u>is</u> green.

Somos muy altos. = <u>We are</u> very tall.

For more words for <u>appearance</u> and <u>personality</u>, see p.14.

5) <u>Personality</u>:

Eres perezoso. = <u>You are</u> lazy.   **Es bastante tímida.** = <u>She is</u> quite shy.

"Ser" is for permanent stuff

Two ways of saying "to be" in Spanish is pretty complicated, I'll give you that. Remember the five golden rules above about when to use "ser" and you won't go too far wrong.

'Ser' and 'Estar'

Now that you've learnt when to use "ser", it's time to learn the <u>rules</u> for "<u>estar</u>".

Use **estar** for **temporary** things

Use "<u>estar</u>" to talk about something that <u>may change</u> in the future, like a <u>feeling</u>:

Mi amigo está muy contento hoy. = My friend <u>is</u> very happy today.

The friend is very happy <u>today</u> — that means that <u>tomorrow</u>, he <u>might not</u> be <u>happy</u>, so it's a <u>temporary</u> situation.

It probably <u>won't be cloudy forever</u> so you use "<u>estar</u>". For more on weather, see p.87. → **Está nublado.** = <u>It is</u> cloudy.

Estoy enfermo. = <u>I am</u> ill. ← *Use "<u>estar</u>" with <u>illness</u> because it's <u>likely</u> to <u>change</u> in the future. See p.29-30 for more on being ill.*

You use **estar** for **locations** too

"<u>Estar</u>" is also used to say <u>where</u> someone or something is:

Barcelona está en España. = Barcelona <u>is</u> in Spain.

Estamos en el parque. = <u>We are</u> in the park.

Están en Italia. = <u>They are</u> in Italy.

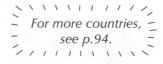
For more countries, see p.94.

For more about how to say where things are, see p.141.

El libro está sobre la mesa. = The book <u>is</u> on the table.

"Estar" is for temporary things and locations

There aren't as many rules to learn for "estar" but you still need to make sure you know them. Not only will using "ser" and "estar" correctly look impressive, but it will get you top marks.

Reflexive Verbs

Reflexive verbs are actions you do to yourself, like "washing yourself".
They're useful if you want to talk about your daily routine in Spanish.

Reflexive verbs have "**se**" on the end

Grammar Fans: these are
"Reflexive verbs".

1) Some infinitives have "se" attached to the end, like "lavarse"
   or "despertarse". These are reflexive verbs.

2) You use a reflexive verb when you want to say that you are doing the action to yourself.

   E.g. "Lavar" means "to wash" but "lavarse" means "to get oneself washed".

   Lavo el perro. = I wash the dog.   **Me lavo**. = I get washed.

3) See p.129 for how to form the reflexive verbs.

Some examples of **reflexive verbs**

Here are some examples of reflexive verbs:

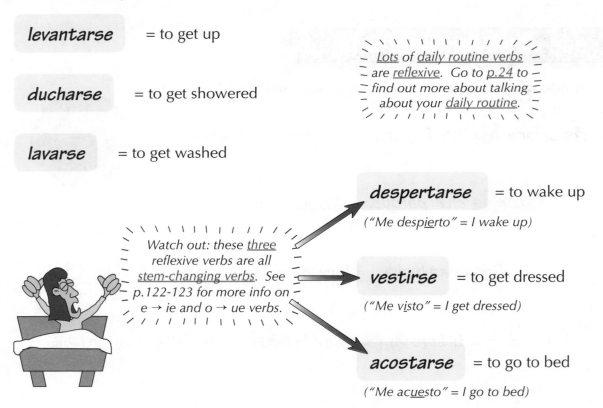

levantarse = to get up

ducharse = to get showered

lavarse = to get washed

Lots of daily routine verbs
are reflexive. Go to p.24 to
find out more about talking
about your daily routine.

despertarse = to wake up

("Me despierto" = I wake up)

Watch out: these three
reflexive verbs are all
stem-changing verbs. See
p.122-123 for more info on
e → ie and o → ue verbs.

vestirse = to get dressed

("Me visto" = I get dressed)

acostarse = to go to bed

("Me acuesto" = I go to bed)

Reflexive verbs are for actions you do to yourself

As you can see, reflexive verbs are really important when you describe your daily routine.
Make sure you know all the verbs on this page and you won't find the next page too tricky.

Reflexive Verbs

This is how to form <u>reflexive verbs</u>. Don't be put off, they're really <u>not</u> as <u>scary</u> as they look.

People doing stuff — **me levanto, me lavo**

The "<u>se</u>" bit (on the infinitive) of reflexive verbs means <u>oneself</u>. This bit <u>changes</u> depending on <u>who is doing the action</u>. Here are all the <u>different ways of saying</u> "<u>se</u>" ("oneself"):

myself =	*me*	*nos*	= ourselves
yourself =	*te*	*os*	= yourselves
himself / herself / itself =	*se*	*se*	= themselves

This is an <u>example</u> of how a <u>reflexive verb</u> looks:

The <u>endings</u> for <u>reflexive verbs</u> are the <u>same</u> as the <u>endings</u> for <u>regular verbs</u>. See p.120-121.

	lavarse = to get washed		
I get washed =	*me lavo*	*nos lavamos*	= we get washed
you (singular) get washed =	*te lavas*	*os laváis*	= you (plural) get washed
he / she / it gets washed =	*se lava*	*se lavan*	= they get washed

How to form **reflexive verbs**

This example is for "<u>I get up</u>":

1 Move "<u>se</u>" <u>in front</u> of the verb.

levant<u>arse</u> ⟹ se + levantar

infinitive

2 <u>Change</u> "<u>se</u>" to the <u>right part</u>.

se + levantar ⟹ <u>me</u> + levantar

3 <u>Change</u> the <u>ending</u> of "<u>levantar</u>" to <u>match the person</u>.

me + levantar ⟹ me + levant<u>o</u> | me levanto | = I get up.

Remember to move the "se" part in front of the verb

Reflexive verbs can seem daunting to start with, but if you split them up into the "se" bit and the verb, they're okay. Write down your daily routine without looking back at this page.

Making Sentences Negative

Even if you have an optimistic outlook on life, you need to know how to form negative sentences.

Use "no" to say not

1) If you want a sentence to have the opposite meaning in English, you add "not".

I'm happy.   **I'm not happy.**

2) In Spanish, if you want a sentence to mean the opposite, put "no" in front of the verb.

Soy bajo. = I'm short.   **No soy bajo.** = I'm not short.

You do the same with all verbs

Make sure you remember to put the "no" before the verb.

Juego al rugby. = I play rugby.

No juego al rugby. = I don't play rugby.

Ed baila bien. = Ed dances well.

The "no" goes before the verb wherever it is in the sentence.

Ed no baila bien. = Ed doesn't dance well.

Puedo venir. = I can come.

No puedo venir. = I can't come.

Me gusta el café. = I like coffee.

No me gusta el café. = I don't like coffee.

"No" always goes before the verb
If you think about it, it's a lot easier to make a sentence negative in Spanish than it is in English. You just have to put the "no" before the verb and you have a negative sentence. Easy.

Making Sentences Negative

Now learn to say other types of <u>negative sentences</u> — sentences with "<u>never</u>" and "<u>nothing</u>".

Never = **nunca**

Here's how to use "<u>nunca</u>":

No + VERB + nunca

No voy nunca al cine.   = I <u>never</u> go to the cinema.

No ayuda nunca a su madre.   = She <u>never</u> helps her mother.

No vemos nunca la televisión.   = We <u>never</u> watch television.

It would also be <u>correct</u> to say "<u>nunca voy al cine</u>", "<u>nunca ayuda a su madre</u>" or "<u>nunca vemos la televisión</u>". See <u>p.144</u> for more.

Nothing = **nada**

And here's how to use "<u>nada</u>":

No + VERB + nada

No hay nada aquí.   = There's <u>nothing</u> here.

No dicen nada.   = They don't say <u>anything</u>.
(Literally: "They say <u>nothing</u>".)

"<u>No</u>" always goes <u>before</u> the verb and "<u>nada</u>" goes <u>after</u> the verb. "<u>Nunca</u>" can change position.

No hace nada.   = He doesn't do <u>anything</u>.
(Literally: "He does <u>nothing</u>.")

Put "no...nunca" or "no...nada" around the verb

Saying "never" and "nothing" in Spanish isn't too bad. Just find the verb and then put "no... nunca/nada" around it, e.g. "<u>no</u> canto <u>nunca</u>" (I never sing) or "<u>no</u> hago <u>nada</u>" (I do nothing).

Talking about the Future

To form the future tense, you need to know "ir" really well. Go back to p.124 if you're not sure.

What is the **future tense**?

1) You use the future tense to talk about events that are going to happen in the future.

2) There are two ways to talk about the future in Spanish. This one, you'll be pleased to know, is the easy way. You can look forward to a different way at GCSE.

You can use "**I'm going to**" to talk about the **future**

To form the future tense, there are three easy parts:

> ### "ir" in the present tense + a + INFINITIVE

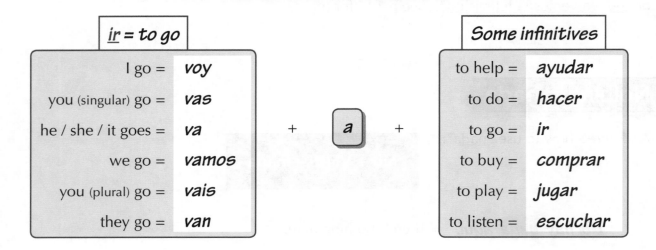

ir = to go	
I go =	*voy*
you (singular) go =	*vas*
he / she / it goes =	*va*
we go =	*vamos*
you (plural) go =	*vais*
they go =	*van*

+ **a** +

Some infinitives	
to help =	*ayudar*
to do =	*hacer*
to go =	*ir*
to buy =	*comprar*
to play =	*jugar*
to listen =	*escuchar*

Van a jugar al ajedrez.   = <u>They are going to play</u> chess.

Voy a hacer mis deberes.   = <u>I am going to do</u> my homework.

¿**Vas a ir** al cine hoy?   = <u>Are you going to go</u> to the cinema today?

Use the future tense to talk about your future holidays

You'll know how to say "I'm going to go to France", "I'm going to swim in the sea" and "I'm going to go with my mother and father" now. Practise saying these sentences with a friend.

Practice Questions

1 Write down whether each sentence below uses 'ser' or 'estar'.

a) She is Spanish.
b) He is my brother.
c) I am ill.
d) His eyes are green.
e) My mother is sad today.
f) David is a policeman.
g) Cara is in Valencia.
h) He is intelligent.

2 Copy and complete these sentences using the correct form of either 'ser' or 'estar'.

a) My uncle is a mechanic. = Mi tío .... mecánico.
b) He is hardworking. = ... trabajador.
c) I am ill. = ... enfermo.
d) They are in the restaurant. = ... en el restaurante.
e) Her eyes are blue. = Sus ojos .... azules.
f) Grizebeck is in England. = Grizebeck .... en Inglaterra.
g) You (singular) are sporty. = ... deportista.
h) This is my mother. = Esta .... mi madre.

3 Copy and complete these reflexive verbs by choosing the correct pronoun from the box.

a) .... levanto
b) .... vestimos
c) .... duchas
d) .... acuestan
e) .... despertáis
f) .... lava

me	nos
te	os
se	se

4 Write these sentences in Spanish. Use the verbs in brackets to help.

a) You (plural) get washed. *[lavarse]*
b) I clean my teeth. *[lavarse los dientes]*
c) You (singular) have a shower. *[ducharse]*
d) We get up *[levantarse]*
e) He goes to sleep. *[acostarse]*
f) They get dressed. *[vestirse]*

HINT: 'acostarse' changes its stem from 'o' to 'ue' and 'vestirse' changes its stem from 'e' to 'i'.

Practice Questions

5 Read the following information about Sara, then write 'true' or 'false' for each statement.

> Me llamo Sara. Soy española. Mi mejor amiga es francesa pero no hablo francés. Me gusta escuchar música y bailar. No me gusta ver películas y no voy nunca al cine. Vivo en un pueblo pequeño y aburrido, pero me gusta mi casa.

a) Sara isn't Spanish.

b) Sara doesn't speak French.

c) She likes listening to music and dancing.

d) She never goes to the cinema.

e) She lives in a large town.

f) She doesn't like her house.

6 Make the following sentences negative. Use the example to help you.
Example: Soy profesora. *No soy profesora.*

a) Me lavo los dientes

b) Tenemos dinero.

c) Mi hermano es alto.

d) Van al cine.

7 Copy and complete the sentences by filling in the gaps with either 'nunca' or 'nada'.

a) No voy .... a la piscina. *[I never go to the swimming pool.]*

b) No hablamos .... en clase. *[We never talk in class.]*

c) No como .... para el desayuno. *[I don't eat anything for breakfast.]*

d) No me escuchas .... *[You never listen to me.]*

e) No hace .... los lunes. *[He doesn't do anything on Mondays.]*

8 Copy and complete these sentences by translating the bits in brackets into Spanish.

a) *[You (plural) are going to]* hacer los deberes.

b) *[We are going to]* hacer esquí.

c) *[They are going to]* jugar al baloncesto.

d) *[You (singular) are going to]* lavar el coche.

e) *[I am going to]* escuchar la radio.

f) *[He is not going to]* hacer footing.

Giving People Orders

Even if you don't give out many <u>orders</u> yourself, you're <u>likely</u> to hear your <u>teacher</u> saying these.

This is how to **give informal orders**

Grammar Fans: this is called the "<u>Imperative</u>".

To give orders in Spanish, just <u>take the "s"</u> off the "<u>you (singular)</u>" part of the verb.
These are <u>informal commands</u> for <u>one person</u> that you <u>know well</u>, like <u>family</u> and <u>friends</u>.

Present tense "you"	Command

hablas ⟹ *¡habla!*

(you speak)　　(speak!)

> *In Spanish, if there's an <u>exclamation mark</u> at the end of a sentence, you also need an <u>upside down</u> exclamation mark (¡) at the start.*

Some <u>examples</u>:

comes ⟹ *¡come!*

(you eat)　　(eat!)

¡Ayuda a tu hermano!　= <u>Help</u> your brother!

¡Bebe el agua!　= <u>Drink</u> the water!

escribes ⟹ *¡escribe!*

(you write)　　(write!)

¡Escribe tu nombre!　= <u>Write</u> your name!

Some **irregular informal orders**

As always, there are some <u>really important irregular</u> ones to learn.

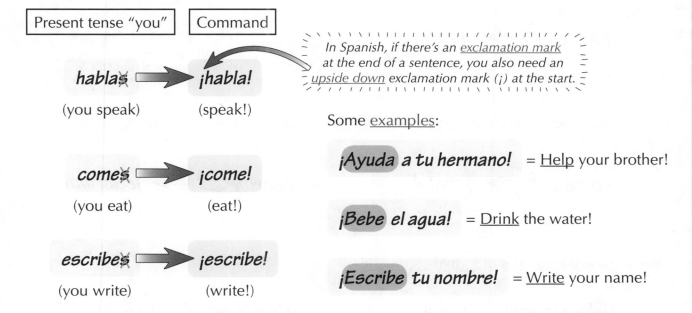

hacer ⟹ *¡haz!* = do!　　　　*ser* ⟹ *¡sé!* = be!

venir ⟹ *¡ven!* = come!　　　*ir* ⟹ *¡ve!* = go!

tener ⟹ *¡ten!* = have!　　*You might see "ten" in set phrases, e.g. "¡ten cuidado!" ("take care!").*

¡Haz tus deberes!

Just knock the "s" off the "you (singular)" part

Even though you won't give many commands yourself, informal commands are fairly easy.
The irregular ones are tricky but they're still important so make sure you learn them anyway.

Giving People Orders

You use <u>formal orders</u> with an <u>adult</u> or a <u>stranger</u>.

Politely tell someone what to do

The endings for politely telling someone what to do are a bit different.
For -<u>ar</u> verbs, take the "<u>he/she/it</u>" form of the <u>present tense</u> and <u>swap</u> the final "<u>a</u>" for an "<u>e</u>".

habla ← e → ¡hable!
= speak!

Luckily for you, for telling more than one person what to do, you'll have to wait until GCSE.

For -<u>er</u> and -<u>ir</u> verbs, take the <u>present tense</u> "<u>he/she/it</u>" form and <u>swap</u> the last "<u>e</u>" for an "<u>a</u>".

come ← a → ¡coma!
= eat!

escribe ← a → ¡escriba!
= write!

Here are some <u>examples</u> of <u>formal commands</u>:

¡Beba el zumo! = <u>Drink</u> the juice!

¡Mire la carta! = <u>Look</u> at the letter!

Some **irregular formal** commands

hacer ⟹ ¡haga! = do!

ser ⟹ ¡sea! = be!

venir ⟹ ¡venga! = come!

ir ⟹ ¡vaya! = go!

tener ⟹ ¡tenga! = have!

Use these polite commands with an adult or stranger

It's really worth taking a bit of time to learn these formal commands. Someone might politely tell you to come somewhere and if you don't understand "¡venga!" you'll be really confused.

Talking about the Past

Here's how to <u>talk about the past</u> — it's just as <u>important</u> as being able to talk about the future.

Use the **past tense** to talk **about the past**

Grammar Fans: this is called the "<u>Preterite Tense</u>".

This is <u>how to form</u> the <u>past tense</u> in Spanish:

① *Find the verb stem by removing the last two letters of the infinitive.*

② *Add on the new ending.*

For more on the infinitive and verb stems, see p.120.

Use these **endings**

Here are the <u>past tense endings</u> (-<u>ir</u> and -<u>er</u> endings are the <u>same</u>):

Endings for -<u>ar</u> verbs, e.g. <u>habl</u>ar (to speak)

I spoke =	*hablé*	*hablamos*	= we spoke
you (singular) spoke =	*hablaste*	*hablasteis*	= you (plural) spoke
he / she / it spoke =	*habló*	*hablaron*	= they spoke

Habló con Ana. = <u>He spoke</u> to Ana.

For the <u>formal</u> "<u>you</u>" (<u>singular</u>), use the "<u>he/she/it</u>" part of the verb and for the <u>formal</u> "<u>you</u>" (<u>plural</u>), use the "<u>they</u>" part.

Endings for -<u>er</u> and -<u>ir</u> verbs, e.g. <u>com</u>er (to eat)

I ate =	*comí*	*comimos*	= we ate
you (singular) ate =	*comiste*	*comisteis*	= you (plural) ate
he / she / it ate =	*comió*	*comieron*	= they ate

Comí el queso. = <u>I ate</u> the cheese.

Use the past to talk about what happened yesterday

Okay, there's a few endings to learn here but once you've mastered them, you should be able to put any regular verb in the past tense. And believe me, the past tense pops up everywhere.

Talking about the Past

You should know by now that there are always <u>exceptions to the rule</u> when it comes to <u>verbs</u>.

"Ser" and "ir" are the same in the past tense

Here's the verb table for "<u>ser</u>" (to be) and "<u>ir</u>" (to go) in the <u>past tense</u>.

ser (to be) and ir (to go)

I was/went =	**fui**	**fuimos**	= we were/went
you (singular) were/went =	**fuiste**	**fuisteis**	= you (plural) were/went
he / she / it was/went =	**fue**	**fueron**	= they were/went

Don't forget — use the "<u>he/she/it</u>" part to form <u>polite</u> "<u>you</u>" (<u>singular</u>) and the "<u>they</u>" part for <u>polite</u> "<u>you</u>" (<u>plural</u>).

In the past tense, "<u>ser</u>" and "<u>ir</u>" are the <u>same</u>, so you have to look at the <u>context</u> to tell what they <u>mean</u>:

Fui *a la playa —* **fue** *excelente.* = <u>I went</u> to the beach — <u>it was</u> excellent.

"Hacer" is another irregular verb

"<u>Hacer</u>" (to do) is also <u>irregular</u> in the <u>past tense</u>:

hacer (to do)

I did =	**hice**	**hicimos**	= we did
you (singular) did =	**hiciste**	**hicisteis**	= you (plural) did
he / she / it did =	**hizo**	**hicieron**	= they did

Hice *la compra.* = <u>I did</u> the shopping.

Irregular verbs in the past tense are really important

It's annoying that the most commonly used verbs are usually irregular. It just means that you need to work extra hard at learning them and make sure you know all the parts inside out.

Practice Questions

Track 18   Listening Question

1   Rafael has had a busy week.
Listen to what he did on each day and answer the questions in English.

a)   Where did Rafael go with his friends on Monday?

b)   What sport did Rafael play in the park?

c)   On which night did Rafael play with his band?

d)   Which activity did Rafael find boring?

e)   What did Rafael do all day on Sunday?

2   Write down what these informal commands mean in English.
Use the infinitives in the box to help you.

ser = to be	*venir = to come*	*hablar = to speak*
empezar = to start	*hacer = to do*	*caminar = to walk*

a)   ¡Habla!

b)   ¡Camina!

c)   ¡Empieza!

d)   ¡Haz tus deberes!

e)   ¡Sé simpático!

f)   ¡Ven!

3   Use the verb table for 'beber' to write each of these '-er' verbs in the past tense.

a)   Yo *[comer]* patatas fritas.

b)   Ella *[volver]* el dos de mayo.

c)   Nosotros *[perder]* todo el dinero.

d)   ¿Tú *[entender]* el problema?

e)   ¿Vosotros *[aprender]* mucho?

f)   Ellos *[correr]* hasta la playa.

beber = to drink

yo = bebí
tú = bebiste
él / ella = bebió
nosotros = bebimos
vosotros = bebisteis
ellos / ellas = bebieron

4   Write these past tense verbs in Spanish.

a)   I suffered *[sufrir]*

b)   We wrote *[escribir]*

c)   They went up *[subir]*

d)   You (singular) opened *[abrir]*

e)   He decided *[decidir]*

f)   You (plural) lived *[vivir]*

HINT: '-ir' verbs
follow the same
pattern as '-er' verbs
— see the table for
'beber' in Q3.

SECTION EIGHT — GRAMMAR AND USEFUL PHRASES

Useful Small Words

Learn these <u>useful little words</u> and you'll be well on your way to being a <u>Spanish expert</u>.

"a" means "to"

Most of the time, to say "<u>to</u>", you use "<u>a</u>":

Va a Bilbao. = He's going <u>to</u> Bilbao.

Voy a casa. = I'm going (<u>to</u>) home.

Vamos al cine. = We're going <u>to the</u> cinema.

"a" + "<u>el</u>" = "<u>al</u>"
See p.105 for more info.

Use "a" or "en" to say "at"

1) In Spanish "<u>a</u>" can <u>also</u> mean "<u>at</u>": **A las cinco.** = <u>At</u> five o'clock.

2) "<u>En</u>" can mean "<u>at</u>", too: **Estoy en casa.** = I'm <u>at</u> home.

"de" means "from"

"<u>From</u>" is usually written as "<u>de</u>":

"<u>de</u>" + "<u>el</u>" = "<u>del</u>"
For more, see p.105.

Soy de Cumbria. = I'm <u>from</u> Cumbria.

Es del aula. = It's <u>from the</u> classroom.

"de" can also mean "of"

When we say "<u>of</u>", Spanish people say "<u>de</u>":

Una botella de zumo. = A bottle <u>of</u> juice.

(Literally a "sandwich of ham")

Un bocadillo de jamón. = A ham sandwich.

"a", "en" and "de" — three small but important words

Okay, verbs are also very important too, but you'll be glad you've learnt these little words if you want to have a Spanish conversation — they come up all the time. Get them learnt.

Useful Small Words

You need to be able to say <u>where something is</u>, so learn this page.

Say **where something is**

Grammar Fans: these are called "<u>Prepositions</u>".

Remember: you use "<u>estar</u>" when you say <u>where something is</u>.

ON = SOBRE

El libro está sobre *la mesa.*

= The book is <u>on</u> the table.

You can also use '<u>en</u>' for '<u>on</u>' too.

UNDER = DEBAJO DE

El libro está debajo de *la mesa.*

= The book is <u>under</u> the table.

IN = EN

El libro está en *el bolso.*

= The book is <u>in</u> the bag.

NEXT TO = AL LADO DE

El libro está al lado de *la mesa.*

= The book is <u>next to</u> the table.

BEHIND = DETRÁS DE

El libro está detrás de *la mesa.*

= The book is <u>behind</u> the table.

IN FRONT OF = DELANTE DE

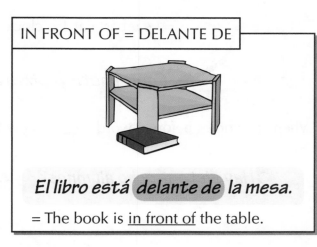

El libro está delante de *la mesa.*

= The book is <u>in front of</u> the table.

Prepositions are useful if you've lost something

If you've lost your pen and your Spanish teacher says, "Está debajo de la silla." you'll be really pleased you learnt this page. If you didn't learn it, there's no chance you'll get your pen back.

Small Linking Words

Learn these little <u>linking words</u> to help you <u>join sentences together</u>.
They're really <u>useful</u> and they work like <u>English linking words</u>.

"Y" means "and"

Grammar Fans: these are called "<u>Conjunctions</u>" or "<u>Connectives</u>".

Use "<u>y</u>" to <u>join</u> two <u>sentences</u> together:

   Desayuna cereales.   AND   **Desayuna fruta.**

= She has cereal for breakfast.   = She has fruit for breakfast.

Desayuna cereales y fruta.   = She has cereal <u>and</u> fruit for breakfast.

Watch out: if "<u>y</u>" comes <u>before</u> a word <u>beginning</u> with "<u>i</u>" or "<u>hi</u>", the "<u>y</u>" <u>changes</u> to an "<u>e</u>":

Estudio español e inglés.   = I study Spanish <u>and</u> English.

"O" means "or"

If you're giving <u>options</u>, you'll need to know how to say "<u>or</u>".

   **Como pasta a la una.**   OR   **Como pizza a la una.**

= I eat pasta at 1 o'clock.   = I eat pizza at 1 o'clock.

Como pasta o pizza a la una.   = I eat pasta <u>or</u> pizza at 1 o'clock.

When "<u>o</u>" comes <u>before</u> a word <u>beginning</u> with "<u>o</u>" or "<u>ho</u>", it <u>changes</u> to "<u>u</u>":

¿Hay siete u ocho alumnos?   = Are there seven <u>or</u> eight pupils?

Your sentences might not make sense if you don't use "and" and "or"

If you never use "and" or "or", I'd be very surprised. They're really useful for joining sentences together. As an added bonus, longer sentences sound loads more impressive, too.

Small Linking Words

Here are some <u>more useful little words</u> for you.

Use "**pero**" for "**but**"

> Don't get "<u>pero</u>" confused with "<u>perro</u>" (dog).

"<u>But</u>" is good for giving an <u>alternative option</u>:

Me gustan las fresas.   BUT   **No me gustan las manzanas.**

= I like strawberries.   = I don't like apples.

Me gustan las fresas (pero) no me gustan las manzanas.

= I like strawberries <u>but</u> I don't like apples.

"**Porque**" means "**because**"

"<u>Porque</u>" is really important for being able to <u>explain yourself</u> and <u>give a reason</u>.

Me gusta esquiar.   BECAUSE   **Es divertido.**

= I like skiing.   = It's fun.

Me gusta esquiar (porque) es divertido.

= I like skiing <u>because</u> it's fun.

Here's <u>another example</u>:

No me gusta jugar al tenis (porque) es difícil.

> For more on opinions, see p.99-100.

= I don't like playing tennis <u>because</u> it's difficult.

Learn to give a reason for your answer

Teachers hate one word answers — fact. The best way to keep them happy is to always give a reason. If you hate chess, say you don't like it because it's difficult (difícil) or boring (aburrido).

How Often

I've said it before and I'll say it again, teachers <u>love it</u> when you include loads of <u>detail</u> in your answers. Learn this page and then you'll be able to say <u>how often</u> you do stuff.

Say **how often** you do things

Grammar Fans: these are called "<u>Adverbs</u>".

The words you use to say <u>how often</u> (or <u>rarely</u>) you do things are called "<u>adverbs</u>". They usually go <u>before</u> the verb. Here are four common ones:

> *never:* nunca
> *rarely:* apenas
> *often:* a menudo
> *always:* siempre

Nunca *hacen los deberes.* = They <u>never</u> do their homework.

"<u>Nunca</u>" and "<u>apenas</u>" can go <u>before</u> the <u>verb</u> (like here). Or, they can <u>also</u> go <u>after</u> the <u>verb</u> if you put "<u>no</u>" <u>before</u> the <u>verb</u>. See p.131 for more ways to use "<u>nunca</u>".

Anabel apenas *juega al hockey.* = Anabel <u>rarely</u> plays hockey.

A menudo *veo la televisión.* = I <u>often</u> watch television.

Siempre *vamos al teatro.* = We <u>always</u> go to the theatre.

Adverbs **don't change** or **agree**

<u>Adverbs</u> always stay the <u>same</u>, even with <u>feminine</u> and <u>plural nouns</u>.

Helena siempre *escucha la radio.*

= Helena <u>always</u> listens to the radio.

Los chicos siempre *escuchan la radio.*

= The boys <u>always</u> listen to the radio.

Adverbs are useful for saying how often you do things

Don't just say "I play football" when you could say "I always play football" or "I often play football". Add how often you do something and you'll sound like a Spanish expert.

How Much

Here are some <u>more words</u> to help you add <u>more detail</u> to your sentences.

"Muy" and "bastante" — "very" and "quite"

Use these words to say <u>how much</u> something is done.
For example, instead of saying rugby is "<u>good</u>", say rugby is "<u>quite good</u>", or "<u>very good</u>".

> *very:* muy
> *quite:* bastante

Estoy muy cansado. = I'm <u>very</u> tired.

"<u>Muy</u>" <u>describes</u> the <u>adjective</u> ("cansado").

La película es bastante aburrida. = The film is <u>quite</u> boring.

"<u>Bastante</u>" <u>describes</u> the <u>adjective</u> ("aburrida").

"Demasiado" means "too much"

> *too much:* demasiado

Mi hermano trabaja demasiado. = My brother works <u>too much</u>.

"<u>Too much</u>" here <u>describes the verb</u> —
it shows <u>how much</u> the brother <u>works</u>.

If you use "too much" <u>to describe a noun</u>, "demasiado" <u>agrees</u>.

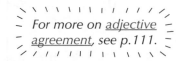

For more on <u>adjective</u> <u>agreement</u>, see p.111.

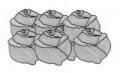

Hay demasiada lechuga. = There's <u>too much</u> lettuce.

"<u>Too much</u>" here <u>describes the noun</u> —
it shows <u>how much</u> lettuce there is.

Estoy muy cansado — estudio demasiado

These three words may only be small, but they'll make your work sound really good. Practise saying or writing as many sentences as you can that include one or more of these words.

Practice Questions

1 Copy and complete these sentences using either 'a' or 'de'.

a) Compré dos botellas .... agua. *[I bought two bottles of water.]*

b) Un kilo .... patatas, por favor. *[A kilo of potatoes, please.]*

c) Tengo una clase .... las dos. *[I've got a class at two o'clock.]*

d) El tren sale .... las seis y media. *[The train leaves at half past six.]*

2 Complete these sentences by translating the preposition in brackets into Spanish.

a) El gato está *[on]* la mesa.

b) El gato está *[in]* la casa.

c) El gato está *[in front of]* la mesa.

d) El gato está *[behind]* la mesa.

e) El gato está *[under]* la mesa.

f) El gato está *[next to]* la mesa.

3 Copy and complete these sentences using either 'pero' or 'porque'.

a) Me gusta estudiar español .... es interesante.

b) Juego al hockey .... no juego al rugby.

c) Me gusta ir al cine .... prefiero ir al teatro.

d) Estudio matemáticas .... quiero ser profesor de matemáticas.

4 Copy and complete these sentences with the correct word from the box.

a) .... haces footing. *[You always go jogging.]*

b) .... veo la televisión. *[I often watch TV.]*

c) .... va al teatro. *[She rarely goes to the theatre.]*

d) .... toca la flauta. *[He never plays the flute.]*

| a menudo |
| apenas |
| siempre |
| nunca |

5 Rewrite these sentences adding the correct word to give more detail.
Use the words in the box to help you.
Example: Ana está contenta. *[Ana is <u>very</u> happy.]* **Ana está muy contenta.**

a) David está cansado. *[David is <u>very</u> tired.]*

b) Susana es alta. *[Susana is <u>quite</u> tall.]*

c) Jaime come. *[Jaime eats <u>too much</u>.]*

d) Gabriela habla. *[Gabriela talks <u>too much</u>.]*

| muy |
| bastante |
| demasiado |

Summary questions

There's loads of grammar in this section and it's really important that you know it, so take your time and answer all of the questions. Then you'll deserve some chocolate. Or maybe you'd prefer something more Spanishy, like a paella, now that you're a Spanish expert...

1) How would you say these in Spanish? a) I love to swim because it's fun.
b) I hate French because it's difficult.

2) Write a question in Spanish using each of these question words:
a) ¿qué?   b) ¿cómo?   c) ¿dónde?   d) ¿cuánto?

3) Turn these Spanish words into plurals: a) la camisa   b) el brazo   c) el lápiz

4) Copy and complete these tables for "the", "a" and "some":

THE	MASCULINE	FEMININE
SINGULAR		
PLURAL		

A	
MASCULINE	FEMININE

SOME	
MASCULINE	FEMININE

5) Rewrite each sentence, replacing the underlined nouns with the correct pronoun:
a) <u>Tomás y Pedro</u> limpian la casa.   b) Vanessa y Helen compran <u>las galletas</u>.

6) Reinaldo wants a new hat. How would he say this in Spanish?

7) Reinaldo reckons his new hat is the best. How would he say this in Spanish?

8) In Spanish, how would Reinaldo say "That hat is my hat."

9) That's enough about Reinaldo's hat. What do these sentences mean in English?
a) Fui por el mercado por la mañana.
b) Quiero ir a Cumbria para hacer ciclismo para un mes.

10) "Ayudar" (to help) is a regular -ar verb. How would you say: a) I help b) he helps c) we help

11) What do these mean in English? a) quiero b) podemos c) tienes d) pueden e) queréis

12) Write these in English: a) vas b) voy c) vais d) van e) va f) vamos

13) a) "Ser" means "to be". Say these using "ser": i) I am ii) you (plural) are iii) he is iv) they are
b) "Estar" also means "to be". Using "estar", what is: i) I am ii) she is iii) we are iv) they are

14) How would you say "there is a mouse in my shoe" in Spanish? Now say "it's big".

15) Write these in Spanish: a) I'm Scottish b) He's kind c) They're sad today d) We're in Madrid

16) Use "ducharse" to write: a) I get showered b) he gets showered c) we get showered

17) Write these in Spanish: a) He can't come b) I never eat rice c) I don't drink anything

18) What are these in English? a) Voy a ir al parque b) Van a cenar c) Vamos a ayudar a mi tío

19) Your teacher says, "¡Escribe tu nombre!". What is he/she telling you to do?

20) How do you say: a) I went to the cinema — it was boring b) They did their homework

21) What's the Spanish for: a) I'm going to Wales b) He's from Cheshire c) A cheese sandwich

22) What do these mean: a) el perro está sobre la mesa b) el perro está delante del sofá

23) In Spanish, write: a) I like geography and German b) I listen to the radio or watch television

24) What do these mean: a) Nunca voy al cine b) Siempre escucha música c) Comen demasiado

Page 5

1) a) Clock 2
   b) Clock 6
   c) Clock 3
   d) Clock 5
   e) Clock 1
   f) Clock 4

2) a) tres + dos = cinco
   b) siete – uno = seis
   c) ocho + cuatro = doce
   d) dieciocho + dos = veinte
   e) catorce – trece = uno
   f) quince – dos = trece

3) a) Friday
   b) Sunday
   c) Wednesday
   d) Thursday
   e) Tuesday
   f) Saturday
   g) On Fridays
   h) Monday
   i) the weekend

4) a) el diecisiete de septiembre
   b) el veintidós de noviembre
   c) el catorce de junio
   d) el dos de marzo
   e) el veintiuno de julio
   f) el primero de enero

Page 11

1) a) False
   b) True
   c) True
   d) True
   e) False

2) a) Buenas noches
   b) Buenas tardes
   c) Hasta luego
   d) ¿Qué tal?
   e) Adiós

3) a) Let me introduce my brother.
   b) This is my friend.
   c) Pleased to meet you.
   d) Let me introduce my mother.

4) a) ¿Puedo comer galletas?
   b) ¿Puedo beber leche?
   c) ¿Puedo ver la televisión?
   d) ¿Puedo poner la mesa?
   e) ¿Puedo escuchar música?
   f) ¿Puedo jugar al fútbol?

Page 19

1)
   Mother — Juana   Aunt — Inés
   Stepfather — Pablo   Cousin — Fernando
   Sister — Alicia   Dog — Max
   Brother — Enrique   Cat — Félix

2) a) Me llamo Jasmine. Soy baja. Tengo los ojos marrones y el pelo rubio.
   b) Me llamo David. Tengo los ojos azules y el pelo negro. Llevo gafas.
   c) Me llamo Sophie. Soy de talla mediana. Soy delgada y tengo el pelo largo.
   d) Me llamo Gareth. Soy gordo. Soy pelirrojo. No llevo gafas.

3) a) a dog
   b) a horse
   c) a bird
   d) a mouse

Pages 26-27

1) a) False
   b) True
   c) False
   d) True

2) a) False   b) True   c) False

3) a) False   b) False   c) True

4) a) el cuarto de baño
   b) el dormitorio
   c) el jardín
   d) el comedor
   e) la cocina
   f) el salón

5) a) una mesa
   b) un sofá
   c) una cama
   d) una silla
   e) un armario
   f) un sillón

6) a) un piso / un apartamento
   b) una casa
   c) un pueblo
   d) una ciudad

7) Inés: Vivo en el noroeste de España.
   Carlos: Vivo cerca del mar.
   Patricia: Vivo en el este de España.
   Sergio: Vivo en el sur de España.

8) a) Ceno.
   b) Desayuno.
   c) Me levanto.
   d) Me despierto.
   e) Me visto.
   f) Me acuesto.

9) a) Lavo los platos.
   b) Paso la aspiradora.
   c) Arreglo mi dormitorio.
   d) Hago mi cama.
   e) Pongo la mesa.

10) a) Los lunes hago mi cama y arreglo mi dormitorio.
    b) Los martes paso la aspiradora y hago la compra.
    c) Pongo la mesa y lavo los platos.
    d) No hago nada. Soy muy perezoso.

Page 31

1) a) the flu
   b) knees and back
   c) the hospital
   d) plasters and some syrup
   e) the pharmacy

2) a) la cabeza
   b) el cuerpo

3) a) el pelo
   b) el brazo
   c) la mano
   d) el estómago
   e) la pierna
   f) el pie

4) a) unas pastillas
   b) una tirita
   c) una crema
   d) un jarabe

5) a) Me duele la garganta.
   b) Me duelen los ojos.
   c) Me duelen los oídos.
   d) Me duele el estómago.
   e) Me duele la cabeza.
   f) Me duelen los pies.

Page 38

1)

Subject	Like	Dislike
Maths		✓
Geography	✓	
Chemistry		✓
German	✓	
Art	✓	
History		✓

2) a) la historia
   b) la física
   c) el alemán
   d) la biología
   e) la educación física
   f) la informática
   g) el francés
   h) las ciencias
   i) la religión

3) a) Me levanto a las ocho.
   b) Las clases empiezan a las nueve.
   c) Las clases terminan a las cuatro y media.
   d) Tenemos ocho clases por día.
   e) Hacemos una hora de deberes por día.

4) b) una profesora = a teacher (female)
   c) un cuaderno = an exercise book
   d) un horario = a timetable
   e) una clase = a lesson
   f) una regla = a ruler

Page 42

1) a) Mechanic
   b) His sister
   c) Doctor

2) a) Secretary
   b) Dentist
   c) Her aunt

3) a) 4
   b) 7
   c) 1
   d) 5
   e) 3
   f) 6
   g) 2

4) a) Quiero ser médico porque es útil.
   b) Quiero ser dentista porque es interesante.
   c) Quiero estudiar inglés porque es fácil.
   d) Quiero ser ingeniero porque ganan mucho dinero.
   e) Quiero estudiar dibujo porque es divertido.

Page 48

1) a) 3   b) 4   c) 1

2) a) Is it far from here?   c) It's nearby.
   b) It's three kilometres away.   d) It's far away.

3) a) la tienda de comestibles   d) la carnicería
   b) el banco   e) la librería
   c) la farmacia   f) la pastelería

4) a) En mi pueblo/ciudad, hay un castillo.
   b) Hay un ayuntamiento y una iglesia.
   c) Hay un museo y un parque.
   d) No hay piscina.
   e) No hay estación en mi pueblo/ciudad.
   f) Hay un cine y un teatro.

Page 57-58

1) mushrooms
chicken
onions
pears
chocolate
wine

2) a) la patata   e) los guisantes
   b) la zanahoria   f) las judías
   c) la coliflor   g) el champiñón
   d) el tomate   h) la cebolla

3) té = tea
café con leche = coffee with milk
chocolate caliente = hot chocolate
vino tinto = red wine
vino blanco = white wine
cerveza = beer
limonada = lemonade
agua mineral = mineral water
zumo de naranja = orange juice

4) a) los cereales   e) el bocadillo
   b) las patatas fritas   f) el pan
   c) el arroz   g) la pasta
   d) la sopa   h) la hamburguesa

5) Likes: ice cream, chocolate, strawberries, pears, bananas
Dislikes: lettuce, cauliflower, peas, steak

6) a) TOM: Ben, ¿tienes sed?
   BEN: No, no tengo sed.
   b) ABI: Meg, ¿tienes hambre?
   MEG: Sí, tengo hambre.

7) a) Desayuno a las ocho.   d) Como un bocadillo de jamón.
   b) Como cereales y bebo café.   e) Ceno a las siete y cuarto.
   c) Almuerzo a las doce y media.   f) Como pollo, arroz y zanahorias.

8) a) el camarero (male), la camarera (female)
   b) la carta   e) el postre
   c) el primer plato   f) el restaurante
   d) la cuenta   g) el plato principal

Page 63

1) a) Black   c) Blue
   b) A jumper   d) 65 euros

2) a) los pantalones   f) el sombrero
   b) el jersey   g) el vestido
   c) la camisa   h) la chaqueta
   d) los calcetines   i) la camiseta
   e) la falda   j) los zapatos

3) a) Llevo una falda verde, un jersey naranja, un sombrero azul, unos zapatos rojos y unos calcetines amarillos.
   b) Llevo unos pantalones rojos, una camisa rosa, una corbata blanca, una chaqueta marrón, unos calcetines negros y unos zapatos grises.

4) a) 5   c) 6   e) 3
   b) 4   d) 2   f) 1

Page 70

1) a) cycling   d) the television
   b) books   e) the piano and the flute
   c) football   f) newspapers

2) a) Juego   d) Juego
   b) Toco   e) Juego
   c) Toco

3) a) Toco el violoncelo.   c) Juego al rugby.
   b) Juego al baloncesto.   d) Toco la batería.

4) a) Me gusta hacer ciclismo porque es fácil.
   b) No me gusta hacer senderismo porque es aburrido.
   c) Me encanta hacer aerobic porque es divertido.
   d) Odio hacer footing porque es difícil.

5) a) Me gusta esta película.   c) Me gusta este libro.
   b) No me gusta esta película.   d) No me gusta este libro.

Page 78-79

1) a) The park   d) 7 o'clock
   b) The cinema   e) 5 euros
   c) In front of the town hall

2) a) 9.30   d) Return ticket, second class
   b) Platform 4   e) 15 euros
   c) 11.15

3) a) el restaurante   e) el cine
   b) la piscina   f) el polideportivo
   c) el teatro   g) mi casa
   d) el parque

4)

Person	Meeting Place	Time
Rubén	in the town centre	10.45
Carmen	**at the theatre**	**8.30**
Iker	**in front of the cinema**	**9.00**
Yolanda	**in front of the swimming pool**	**10.15**
Patricio	**at Patricio's house**	**3.00**

5)

Spanish	English
el autobús	**bus**
el autocar	coach
el avión	**plane**
el barco	boat
el coche	car
el metro	**the underground**
la motocicleta	motorbike
la bicicleta	**bike**

6) a) Quisiera un billete de ida / sencillo, de primera clase, para Segovia.
   b) Quisiera un billete de ida y vuelta, de primera clase, para Ávila.
   c) Quisiera un billete de ida y vuelta, de segunda clase, para Cuenca.

Page 85

1) a) una carta = a letter
   b) una postal = a postcard
   c) un buzón = a postbox
   d) la dirección = the address
   e) un sobre = an envelope

2) a) <u>Gracias</u> por tu <u>carta</u>. d) ¿Qué <u>tal</u>?

   b) <u>Querido</u> John, e) <u>Escríbeme</u> pronto.

   c) Un <u>abrazo</u>.

3) Answer should follow the following model:

Hometown

19 de septiembre

Querida Ana,

¿Qué tal? Gracias por tu carta.

Me alegró mucho oír de ti. Escríbeme pronto.

Saludos

Jane

4) a) 1 c) 3

   b) 4 d) 5

Page 92-93

1) North: A) and G)

   East: D) and H)

   West: C)

   South: E) and F)

2) a) False c) False

   b) True d) True

3) a) <u>hace</u> sol d) <u>está</u> nevando

   b) <u>está</u> lloviendo e) <u>hay</u> tormenta

   c) <u>hace</u> calor f) <u>está</u> nublado

4) a) Julio es un mes en <u>el verano</u>.

   b) Diciembre es un mes en <u>el invierno</u>.

   c) Octubre es un mes en <u>el otoño</u>.

   d) Abril es un mes en <u>la primavera</u>.

5) a) la caravana d) la tienda

   b) el saco de dormir e) la parcela

   c) el agua potable

6) a) To the south of Portugal

   b) Her mother, stepfather and brother

   c) By car

   d) 2 weeks

   e) In a hotel

   f) It's very hot

7) b) una habitación doble con balcón

   c) una habitación individual con baño

   d) una habitación doble con ducha

8) a) ¿Tiene una parcela libre?

   b) Quisiera una parcela para una caravana.

   c) Quisiera una parcela para una tienda.

   d) Quisiera quedarme cinco noches.

9) a) Emma c) Peter

   b) Peter d) Emma

Page 97

1) a) Holland d) Switzerland

   b) Germany e) Belgium

   c) Ireland

2) a) Vivo en Italia. c) Vivo en España.

   b) Vivo en Portugal. d) Vivo en Austria.

3) a) inglés (m) inglesa (f)

   b) norirlandés (m) norirlandesa (f)

   c) escocés (m) escocesa (f)

   d) galés (m) galesa (f)

4) a) Soy inglesa. d) Soy español.

   b) Soy irlandés. e) Soy italiana.

   c) Soy francesa. f) Soy galés.

5) a) False d) False

   b) True e) True

   c) True f) False

Page 103

1) a) Me gusta el dibujo. d) Me encantan las ciencias.

   b) Odio la geografía. e) Me gustan las matemáticas.

   c) No me gusta la informática. f) No me gusta la historia.

2) a) No me gusta el ajedrez porque es difícil.

   b) Me gusta escuchar la radio porque es interesante.

   c) Odio lavar el coche porque es horrible.

   d) Me encantan los deportes porque son divertidos.

3) a) When is your birthday? d) How much does a lemonade cost?

   b) Where does Sandra live? e) What time do you eat?

   c) How is your mother? f) Who is Alexis?

4) a) ¿Dónde vives? d) ¿Cuál es tu número de teléfono?

   b) ¿Cuánto cuesta el libro? e) ¿Cuándo sale el tren?

   c) ¿Cómo vas al instituto? f) ¿Qué hay en tu dormitorio?

Pages 109-110

1) b) dos peras g) dos tomates

   c) dos granjas h) dos clases

   d) dos armarios i) dos vestidos

   e) dos calles j) dos parques

   f) dos bicicletas

2) a) Tengo cuatro <u>hermanas</u>.

   b) Miguel come muchos <u>plátanos</u>.

   c) Mis primos son <u>albañiles</u>.

   d) En mi casa hay seis <u>habitaciones</u>.

   e) En la pastelería hay muchos <u>pasteles</u>.

   f) En nuestro salón tenemos dos <u>sillones</u>.

3) a) la tortuga f) la tirita

   b) las revistas g) los actores

   c) el médico h) el restaurante

   d) las corbatas i) las reglas

   e) el bocadillo j) la trompeta

4) a) El banco está enfrente <u>del</u> supermercado.

   b) El cine está al lado <u>de la</u> farmacia.

   c) Para ir <u>al</u> banco, tome la primera calle <u>a la</u> derecha.

   d) La estación está <u>al</u> final <u>de la</u> calle.

   e) Para ir <u>a la</u> playa, tome la segunda calle <u>a la</u> izquierda.

5) a) No tengo animales en casa c) No tengo bolígrafos.

   b) No tengo hermanos. d) No tengo dinero.

6)

   she — ella

   you (singular) — tú

   I — yo

   we — nosotros

   they (feminine) — ellas

   you (plural) — vosotros

   he — él

   they (masculine) — ellos

7) a) Mi abuela <u>nos</u> visita. c) <u>Te</u> conozco.

   b) Janice y Deborah <u>me</u> ven. d) <u>Os</u> miro.

8) a) Mi madre <u>la</u> limpia. d) Natalia <u>los</u> quiere.

   b) Ellos <u>los</u> lavan. e) Nosotros <u>lo</u> bebemos.

   c) Rafael <u>las</u> compra.

Page 118-119

1) a) False b) False

2) a) True b) False

3) a) True b) True

4) a) Mi casa no es muy <u>grande</u>.

   b) Las sillas son <u>raras</u>.

   c) Mi amiga es <u>inteligente</u>.

   d) Mi hermana es <u>trabajadora</u>.

   e) Estos deberes son <u>difíciles</u>.

f) Mis pantalones son <u>verdes</u> y <u>largos</u>.

g) Mi primo es <u>horrible</u> pero mi tía es <u>simpática</u>.

h) Tengo dos lápices <u>rojos</u> y un bolígrafo <u>negro</u>.

5) Augustín: Me gustan mis tortugas verdes.

    Luisa: Vivo en una casa pequeña.

    Rodolfo: Quiero una pizza grande.

    Ornella: Tengo unos libros buenos.

    Rodrigo: Vamos al cine nuevo.

6) a) ¿Dónde están <u>sus</u> padres?

b) <u>Mis</u> zapatos son muy cómodos.

c) ¿<u>Sus</u> amigos están aquí?

d) <u>Tus</u> libros están en <u>su</u> cama.

e) <u>Mi</u> tío es <u>tu</u> profesor.

7) a) <u>Nuestra</u> abuela es inteligente.

b) <u>Vuestras</u> casas están cerca.

c) <u>Nuestros</u> perros son simpáticos.

d) <u>Vuestros</u> primos viven con <u>nuestras</u> primas.

8)

the book	el libro	the shirt	la camisa
this book	**este libro**	this shirt	esta camisa
that book	ese libro	that shirt	**esa camisa**
these books	**estos libros**	these shirts	**estas camisas**
those books	**esos libros**	those shirts	**esas camisas**

9) a) para   f) para

b) por   g) por

c) para   h) para

d) por   i) por

e) por   j) para

Page 125

1) a) cantamos   f) ayudas

b) asisto   g) bebo

c) corre   h) subimos

d) aprende   i) preparan

e) decidís

2) a) quiere   d) quieres

b) quieren   e) queremos

c) quiero   f) queréis

3) a) tengo   d) tenéis

b) tienen   e) tiene

c) tienes   f) tenemos

4) a) Yo <u>estoy</u> en Madrid.   e) Tú <u>eres</u> alto.

b) Olivia <u>es</u> profesora.   f) Yo <u>voy</u> a la piscina.

c) Iago y Nacho <u>van</u> al cine.   g) Ellos <u>son</u> españoles.

d) Jorge <u>está</u> muy contento.   h) Ana y yo <u>estamos</u> en el parque.

5) a) En mi estuche <u>hay</u> un lápiz que <u>es</u> gris.

b) Mi dormitorio <u>es</u> grande pero la cocina <u>es</u> pequeña.

c) En mi dormitorio <u>hay</u> una cama y una mesa, pero no <u>hay</u> televisión.

d) La historia <u>es</u> muy aburrida pero el inglés <u>es</u> muy interesante.

e) <u>Hay</u> muchos museos en París porque <u>es</u> la capital de Francia.

Page 133-134

1) a) ser   e) estar

b) ser   f) ser

c) estar   g) estar

d) ser   h) ser

2) a) Mi tío <u>es</u> mecánico.   e) Sus ojos <u>son</u> azules.

b) <u>Es</u> trabajador.   f) Grizebeck <u>está</u> en Inglaterra.

c) <u>Estoy</u> enfermo.   g) <u>Eres</u> deportista.

d) <u>Están</u> en el restaurante.   h) Esta <u>es</u> mi madre.

3) a) <u>me</u> levanto   d) <u>se</u> acuestan

b) <u>nos</u> vestimos   e) <u>os</u> despertáis

c) <u>te</u> duchas   f) <u>se</u> lava

4) a) Os laváis.   d) Nos levantamos.

b) Me lavo los dientes.   e) Se acuesta.

c) Te duchas.   f) Se visten.

5) a) False   d) True

b) True   e) False

c) True   f) False

6) a) No me lavo los dientes.   c) Mi hermano no es alto.

b) No tenemos dinero.   d) No van al cine.

7) a) No voy <u>nunca</u> a la piscina.   d) No me escuchas <u>nunca</u>.

b) No hablamos <u>nunca</u> en clase.   e) No hace <u>nada</u> los lunes.

c) No como <u>nada</u> para el desayuno.

8) a) <u>Vais a</u> hacer los deberes.   d) <u>Vas a</u> lavar el coche.

b) <u>Vamos a</u> hacer esquí.   e) <u>Voy a</u> escuchar la radio.

c) <u>Van a</u> jugar al baloncesto.   f) <u>No va a</u> hacer footing.

Page 139

1) a) the cinema   d) going shopping

b) football   e) hiking

c) Thursday

2) a) Speak!   d) Do your homework!

b) Walk!   e) Be kind!

c) Start!   f) Come!

3) a) Yo <u>comí</u> patatas fritas.

b) Ella <u>volvió</u> el dos de mayo.

c) Nosotros <u>perdimos</u> todo el dinero.

d) ¿Tú <u>entendiste</u> el problema?

e) ¿Vosotros <u>aprendisteis</u> mucho?

f) Ellos <u>corrieron</u> hasta la playa.

4) a) sufrí   d) abriste

b) escribimos   e) decidió

c) subieron   f) vivisteis

Page 146

1) a) Compré dos botellas <u>de</u> agua.   c) Tengo una clase <u>a</u> las dos.

b) Un kilo <u>de</u> patatas, por favor.   d) El tren sale <u>a</u> las seis y media.

2) a) sobre   d) detrás de

b) en   e) debajo de

c) delante de   f) al lado de

3) a) Me gusta estudiar español <u>porque</u> es interesante.

b) Juego al hockey <u>pero</u> no juego al rugby.

c) Me gusta ir al cine <u>pero</u> prefiero ir al teatro.

d) Estudio matemáticas <u>porque</u> quiero ser profesor de matemáticas.

4) a) <u>Siempre</u> haces footing.   c) <u>Apenas</u> va al teatro.

b) <u>A menudo</u> veo la televisión.   d) <u>Nunca</u> toca la flauta.

5) a) David está <u>muy</u> cansado.   c) Jaime come <u>demasiado</u>.

b) Susana es <u>bastante</u> alta.   d) Gabriela habla <u>demasiado</u>.

Track 1 Page 5

1) a)

F1: Es la una y veinte.

b)

M1: Son las cuatro y media.

c)

F2: Son las siete menos diez.

d)

M2: Son las once menos cuarto.

e)

F1: Son las nueve y veinticinco.

f)

M1: Es la una menos cinco.

Track 2 Page 11

1)

F1: ¡Hola, Roberto! ¿Qué tal?

M1: Bien, gracias, Cristina. ¿Y tú?

F1: Muy bien. ¿Quieres beber algo?

M1: Quisiera una limonada, por favor.

F1: ¿Y un pastel? Son deliciosos.

M1: Lo siento, Cristina. No me gustan los pasteles. Quisiera un bocadillo por favor.

F1: ¡Claro, Roberto!

Track 3 Page 19

1)

F2: Mira esta foto de mi familia. Ésta es mi madre. Se llama Juana. Y éste es mi padrastro. Se llama Pablo. Mi hermana se llama Alicia. Tiene nueve años. Mi hermano se llama Enrique y tiene quince años. También tengo una tía que se llama Inés y un primo que se llama Fernando. Tengo dos animales en casa. Mi perro se llama Max. Es muy simpático. Mi gato se llama Félix. Es muy gordo.

Track 4 Page 26

1) a)

M1: Me llamo Esteban. Vivo en Segovia, una ciudad en el centro de España. Me gusta vivir aquí porque es bonito.

b)

F2: Me llamo Beatriz. Vivo en Villanueva, un pueblo en el sur de España. Está en el campo. No me gusta vivir aquí porque es muy aburrido.

c)

M2: Me llamo Alfonso. Vivo en Potes, un pueblo en el norte de España. Está en las montañas y me gusta vivir aquí porque es tranquilo.

d)

F1: Me llamo Leticia. Vivo en Barcelona, una ciudad muy grande en el noreste de España. Está cerca del mar. Me gusta mucho vivir aquí porque es divertido.

Track 5 Page 26

2)

M2: Me llamo Miguel. Me levanto a las siete y media y voy al instituto a las ocho. Vuelvo a casa a las cuatro, ceno a las seis y hago mis deberes a las siete. Me acuesto a las nueve y media.

3)

F2: Me llamo Isabel. Me levanto a las seis, me lavo a las seis y cuarto y desayuno a las siete. Por la tarde, ceno a las ocho, veo la televisión a las nueve y me acuesto a las once.

Track 6 Page 31

1)

M1: Me llamo Marc. ¡Estoy enfermo! Me duele la cabeza, me duelen los oídos y me duelen las piernas, también. Creo que tengo la gripe. Quiero ir al médico.

F1: Me llamo Daniela. Me gusta hacer ciclismo pero ahora me duelen las piernas, me duelen las rodillas y me duele la espalda, también. Quiero ir al hospital.

M2: Soy Carlos. ¡No me encuentro bien! Me duelen los dedos y necesito tiritas. Me duele la garganta y necesito un jarabe. Y me duele el estómago, también. Voy a la farmacia.

Track 7 Page 38

1)

M2: En el instituto me gusta el dibujo porque es fácil y me gusta el alemán porque es interesante. No me gusta la química porque es aburrida, no me gustan las matemáticas porque son difíciles y odio la historia – es inútil. Mi asignatura preferida es la geografía porque es divertida.

Track 8 Page 42

1)

M2: Mi padre es mecánico y trabaja en un garaje. Mi madre es enfermera en un hospital. Mi hermana es peluquera y trabaja en una peluquería. En el futuro yo quiero ser médico.

2)

F2: Mi padre es policía. Mi madre es secretaria y trabaja en una oficina. Mi tío es dentista y mi tía es actriz y trabaja en el teatro. Yo quiero ser profesora.

Track 9 Page 48

1) a)

M1: Perdone, señora. ¿Dónde está el polideportivo, por favor?

F1: Tome la segunda calle a la izquierda y está a la derecha.

M1: Muchas gracias.

b)

F2: Perdone. ¿Para ir a la estación de trenes, por favor?

M2: Siga todo recto. No está lejos.

F2: Gracias.

M2: De nada.

c)

M1: Hola señora. ¿Para ir al cine, por favor?

F1: Tome la primera calle a la derecha y está al final de la calle.

M1: Gracias.

Track 10 Page 57

1)

F2: Voy a preparar una cena para ocho personas y necesito muchas cosas. Para el primer plato necesito doscientos gramos de champiñones y para el segundo plato necesito un pollo y unas cebollas. Quiero un kilo de peras y mucho chocolate para el postre. Y, ¿qué vamos a beber? ¿Cerveza? No, voy a comprar un buen vino blanco.

Track 11 Page 63

1)

F1: ¿En qué puedo servirle, señor?

M1: ¿Tiene unos zapatos negros, por favor?

F1: Sí. Aquí tiene. ¿Le gustan?

M1: Sí. Los compro.

F1: Muy bien. ¿Es todo?

M1: No. Quiero un jersey.

F1: ¿De qué color?

M1: Rojo.

F1: Lo siento, señor. No tenemos jerseys rojos pero tenemos jerseys azules. ¿Le gusta este jersey azul?

M1: Sí. Lo compro. ¿Cuánto cuesta todo?

F1: Son sesenta y cinco euros.

M1: Muchas gracias. Adiós.

F1: Adiós, señor.

Track 12 Page 70

1)

F1: Me llamo Alicia. En mi tiempo libre hago ciclismo, leo libros y toco la guitarra. No escucho la radio y no me gusta ver la televisión.

M2: Me llamo Felipe. Me gusta jugar al fútbol con mis amigos y nado en la piscina también. Me gusta mucho ver la televisión pero no leo libros.

F2: Me llamo Begoña. En mi tiempo libre toco el piano y la flauta y me gusta escuchar música. Leo revistas pero no me gusta leer periódicos.

Track 13 Page 78

1)

F2: ¡Hola Andrés!

M2: ¡Hola Luisa! ¡Vamos al parque!

F2: No, no quiero ir. Hace frío.

M2: ¿Quieres ir al cine? Hay una película con Penélope Cruz.

F2: Sí, buena idea. Me gustan las películas de Penélope Cruz. ¿Dónde nos encontramos?

M2: Nos encontramos delante del ayuntamiento a las siete. ¿Está bien?

F2: Sí. ¿Cuánto cuesta una entrada?

M2: Cinco euros.

F2: Muy bien. Hasta luego.

M2: Hasta luego, Luisa.

Track 14 Page 78

2)

M2: ¿Sí, señora?

F1: ¿A qué hora sale el tren para Pamplona, por favor?

M2: Sale a las nueve y media.

F1: ¿De qué andén sale?

M2: Del andén número cuatro.

F1: ¿Y a qué hora llega el tren a Pamplona?

M2: El tren llega a las once y cuarto, señora.

F1: Bueno. Y un billete de ida y vuelta, de segunda clase, ¿cuánto cuesta?

M2: Quince euros, por favor.

Track 15 Page 92

1)

M1: El tiempo para hoy en España. En el norte del país está nevando y hace frío. ¡Lleven sus abrigos! En el este hay tormenta y está lloviendo. Hace muy mal tiempo. En el oeste de España hace viento. En el sur del país hace sol y hace calor. Para la gente del sur, ¡es como un día de verano!

Track 16 Page 92

2)

M1: Buenos días. ¿En qué puedo servirle?

F2: ¿Tiene habitaciones libres, por favor?

M1: ¿Para cuántas noches?

F2: Para tres noches.

M1: Sí, señora. ¿Cuántas habitaciones quiere?

F2: Una habitación doble con baño y dos habitaciones individuales con ducha.

M1: Muy bien.

F2: ¿Cuánto cuesta en total, por favor?

M1: Pues, una habitación doble cuesta ochenta euros la noche. Para dos habitaciones individuales, son ciento veinte euros la noche. El desayuno está incluido.

F2: Muchas gracias.

Track 17 Page 118

1)

M2: Me llamo Santiago. Mi madre es más baja que mi hermana Alejandra y mi padre es más gordo que mi madre. Mi tío Carlos es tan aburrido como mi tío Juan.

2)

F2: Me llamo Teresa. Vivo con mi madre – es muy simpática. Es más simpática que mi padre. Mi hermano Antonio es más alto que mi hermana María, pero María es más inteligente que Antonio.

3)

M1: Me llamo David. Mi hermana Conchita es delgada pero mi madre es más delgada que mi hermana. Mi hermano Enrique es más divertido que mi hermana Conchita.

Track 18 Page 139

1)

F1: Hola, Rafael. ¿Cómo estás?

M2: Estoy muy cansado. Hice muchas cosas la semana pasada.

F1: ¿Qué hiciste?

M2: Bueno, el lunes fui al cine con mis amigos. El martes escuché música hasta muy tarde porque me encanta la música. El miércoles jugué al fútbol en el parque. Fue muy divertido. El jueves toqué la guitarra con mi grupo. Tocamos música rock. Y el viernes fui a nadar dos horas. El sábado fui de compras con mi familia, pero no me gusta ir de compras. Es aburrido. Y el domingo hice senderismo todo el día.

F1: ¿Y qué vas a hacer hoy, Rafael?

M2: ¡Nada! Hoy me quedo en casa.

Index

Index